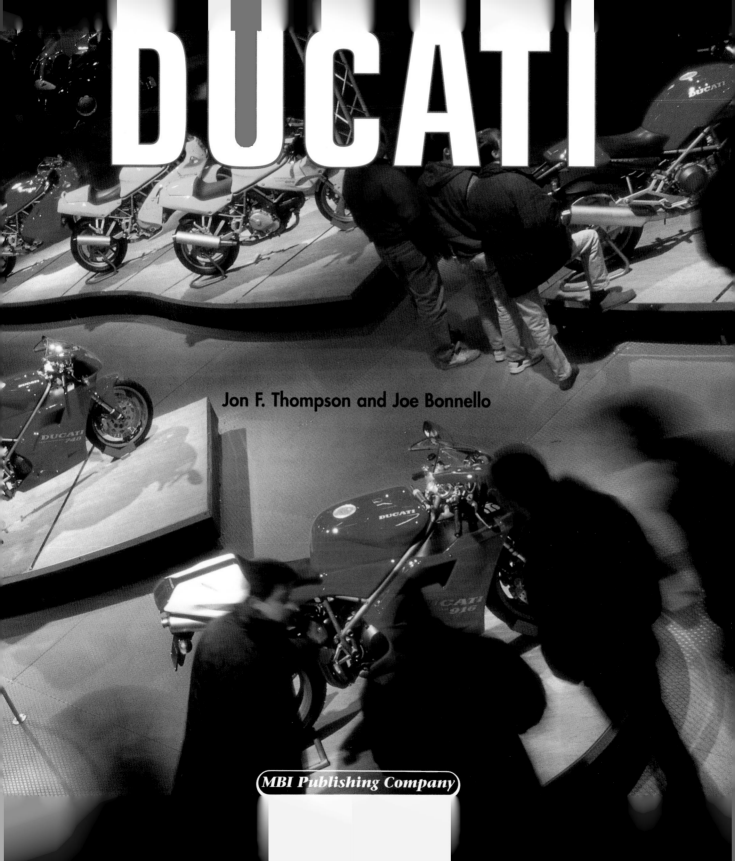

DUCATI

Jon F. Thompson and Joe Bonnello

MBI Publishing Company

First published in 1998 by MBI Publishing Company, 729 Prospect Avenue, PO Box 1, Osceola, WI 54020-0001 USA.

MBI Publishing Company books are also available at discounts in bulk quantity for industrial or sales-promotional use. For details write to Special Sales Manager at Motorbooks International Wholesalers & Distributors, 729 Prospect Avenue, PO Box 1, Osceola, WI 54020-0001 USA.

Library of Congress Cataloging-in-Publication Data

Thompson, Jon F.
    Ducati/ Jon F. Thompson and Joe Bonnello.
        p. cm.-- (Enthusiast color series)
    Includes index.
    ISBN 0-7603-0389-4 (pbk. : alk. paper)
    1. Ducati motorcycle--History. 2. Ducati motorcycle--Pictorial works. I. Bonnello, Joe, 1952- II. Title. III. Series.
TL448.D8T46   1998
629.227'5--dc21   97-45036

Text by Jon F. Thompson
Photos by Joe Bonnello unless credited otherwise

Edited by Lee Klancher
Designed by Katie L. Sonmor

Printed in Hong Kong through World Print, Ltd.

DEDICATION

For Laura, there when I come home from a ride.

ACKNOWLEDGMENTS

I'd like to thank those people quoted here who patiently endured my questions, especially Joe Parkhurst, Phil Schilling, and Mike Berliner. All provided reference points without which this book could not have been done. I also would like to acknowledge historical and background information gleaned from *Ducati: A Retrospective*, an in-house publication of Cagiva North America.
Jon F. Thompson

CONTENTS

INTRODUCTION

Most of us would rather ride Ducatis than read about them. But we can't ride all the time, and that's probably just as well, for we'd be very narrow people indeed if motorcycles were the only things that harnessed our interests.

Nevertheless, there are things about Ducatis, and about the people who build and sell them, that are worth reading about. For this tiny company, which as of this writing has just won its sixth manufacturer's' championship in seven years in World Superbike racing, has had a far greater impact and influence on motorcycling than its tiny size and minuscule production could possibly suggest. So there's no shortage of books about this storied Italian marque.

Unfortunately, none of these books is written from an American perspective. They're written in England or they're written in Italy, from English or Italian perspectives.

That's fine, as far as it goes, but it's also curious, for Ducati has had as much influence in the United States as it's had elsewhere. What is less well acknowledged is that American enthusiasts, and the market that serves them, have had considerable influence on the Italians who design and build Ducatis. So it's especially interesting that very little exists on bookshelves that speaks about Ducatis with an American accent.

This book proposes to change that. It's a project that I find especially interesting, for during my 1988–1995 tenure on the editorial staff of *Cycle World* magazine, I was captured by the Ducati charisma and the intense involvement it produces. As a result of this, at this writing, a pair of Ducatis resides in my garage.

These two bikes are as different as they could be. One's a 1965 350-cc Sebring vintage roadracer that I run in American Historic Racing Motorcycles Association (AHRMA) events. The other is a 1990 851 Strada—the very first one of them to be brought to the United States—that I sport-ride on Sunday mornings, or whenever else I can pry myself away from work. One's a tiny, air-cooled Single with neither lights nor license, a tame little streetbike converted to competition use. The other's a sophisticated streetbike that is, for all its polish, scarcely removed from its fearsome World Superbike racing antecedents. For all the considerable difference between these two, they seem to encapsulate the style and the engineering sophistication that capture the enthusiasm of those who love these charismatic motorcycles from Italy.

Part of the appeal, I think, is that Ducatis are not at all common; in its best year Ducati imported about 7,000 motorcycles to the United States. In its worst year, it imported almost none. A larger part of the marque's appeal involves Ducati's competition heritage, and the fact that the company's streetbikes really aren't far removed from its racebikes. From the very first days of the marque's involvement with the two-wheeled world, Ducati went racing, and did so with surprising brio and technical sophistication, and with amazing success. That racing heritage naturally imbues Ducati streetbikes with a special nimbleness and flair.

Equally seductive, however, is the fact that the company seemingly never has been satisfied with easy, or common, or inexpensive, engineering solutions. That's why tubular frames and desmodromic valve actuation remain Ducati trademarks. The company couldn't shed these trademarks even if it wanted to, as each is seen to be a Ducati mark of identification. Additionally, some of these unique characteristics yield practical attributes that make Ducatis surprisingly easy and comfortable to ride. Despite their high levels of sophistication and performance, these bikes are surprisingly rider-friendly and confidence-building.

But the appeal mostly, I think, is that Ducatis always have been beautiful, designed with all the attention to line and proportion that Italian designers are so famed for. They're as wonderful to look at as they are to ride.

Which brings us back to reading versus riding. I suggest you ride when you can. When you can't, read and think—not only about Ducatis, but about everything that makes life worth living.

Jon F. Thompson
Glendale, California

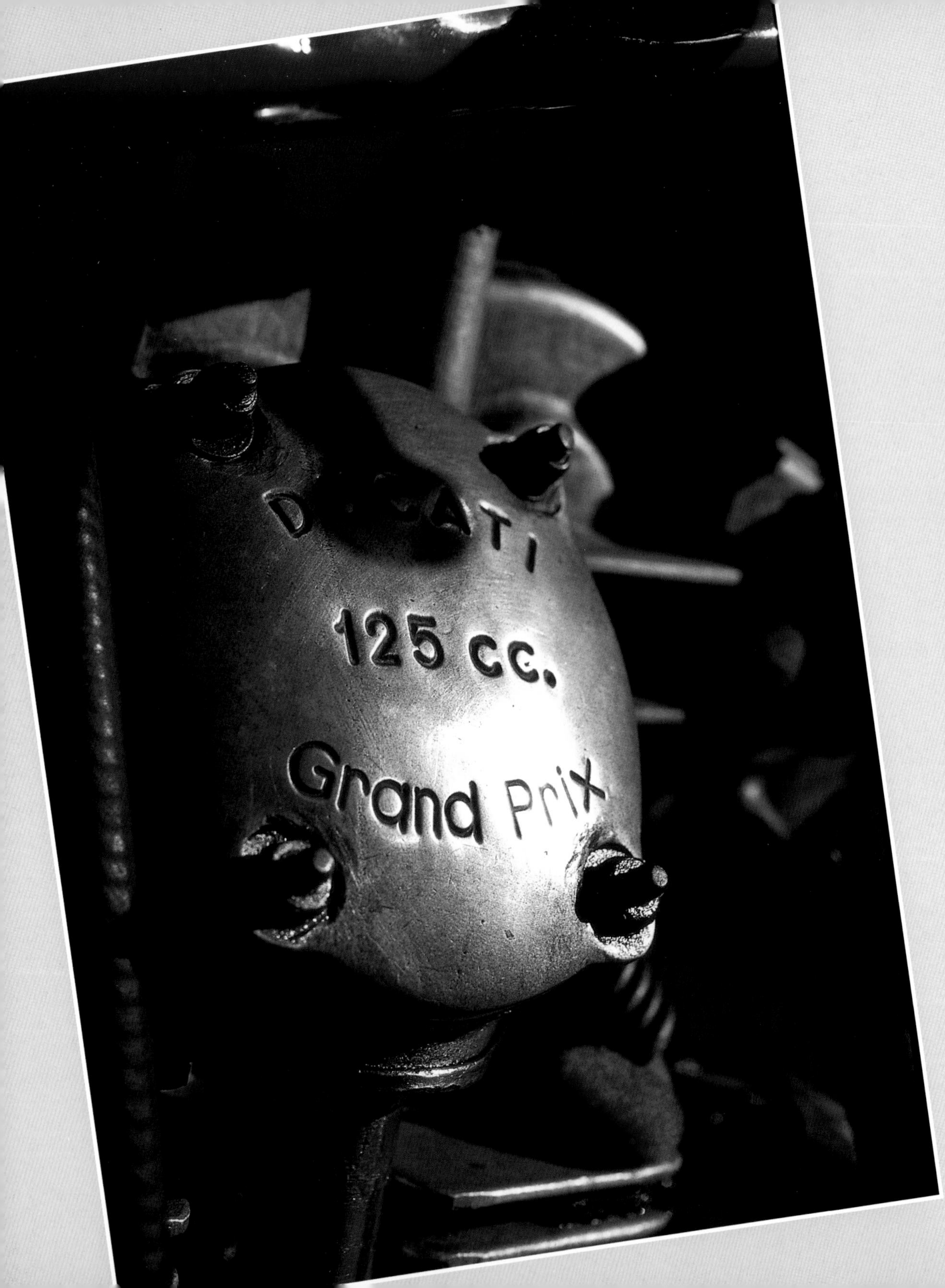
125 cc.
Grand Prix

ONE
FROM RADIO PARTS TO MOTORCYCLES

The story of Ducati is one of fits and starts, of brilliant engineering overseen by Marx Brothers management. It's a story of boom and bust cycles, with Italian managers unable, or unwilling, to deal with the problems of American sales and distribution in a way appropriate to the American market. It's a story of Big Business intermixed with elements of Italian family and Italian government bureaucracy, one that illustrates some of the complexities of intercultural and international business dealings. And ultimately, it's a story that is open-ended, for as this was being written, the announcement came that a complex deal had sold about half the company to American investors David Bonderman, James G. Coulter, and William S. Price. These investors form the Texas Pacific Group, which has interests in the airline, health-care, food, wine, entertainment, telephone, energy, and waste-management industries. It's a company very seriously interested in profits, but not particularly interested in motorcycling.

SETTING THE TONE. Though it is square and later examples are triangular, this cover for the Gran Prix's cam drive, high on top of the bevel-drive shaft on the right side of the engine, illustrates that Taglioni's thinking about engine design, and how to deal with providing access to service areas, was well developed.

THE RAREST OF THE RARE. When Fabio Taglioni created the 125 Gran Prix in 1955 and put it on its first race track in 1956, he couldn't have known that he was creating what would become the rarest of all Ducatis. This fine example is one of the few survivors and is owned by Doug Van Tassel, a private collector and enthusiast in California.

In a way, that's not a bad fit, for it merges with the way Ducati was founded in Bologna in 1926, when brothers Adriano, Bruno, and Marcello Ducati went into business together, not to make motorcycles, but to make money.

The Ducati brothers founded the Societa Scientifica Radiobrevetti Ducati to develop and produce components for radios and other electrical items in Borgo Panigale, a suburb of Bologna. It was a good business to be in. Benito Mussolini and his Fascists, in power since 1922, were eager to consolidate popular support, and because illiteracy was widespread, propaganda was most easily spread by radio, and easy availability of radios was important to the regime.

Business was good, and by 1943 Ducati had about 9,000 workers on its rolls and had graduated from simple radio parts to the manufacture of electronic components for military applications. This made the factory a prime target for Allied bombers, and it was all but destroyed by bombing raids by the time the Fascist Republic of Northern Italy finally collapsed in 1945.

Meanwhile, a thinker named Aldo Farinelli had been pondering Italy's immediate postwar future. He saw that personal transportation would be a top priority. But fuel was scarce and expensive, so much so that bicycles were in wide use and a few Italians took the drastic step of converting their cars to run on homemade fuel distilled from wine.

Farinelli was determined to use the bicycles already in existence to solve the problem of effective transportation. To do that, he turned to the Societa Italiana Applicazioni Techniche Auto-Aviatorie (SIATA), in Turin. His objective was the development of an engine that could be clipped onto a bicycle.

SIATA, which was dedicated to the task of tuning Fiats for sport and racing use, was well equipped for this job. Like the Ducatis' SSRD, it had begun business in 1926. During the war, the company built military vehicles, but Farinelli and SIATA engineers found the time to design their clip-on engine, and had a prototype built and running by 1944. Because the exhaust note of this low-compression, 1-horsepower 48-cc four-stroke engine was a high-pitched bark, Farinelli and his colleagues named it the *Cucciolo*, or puppy. The engine, made mostly of a silicone-aluminum alloy, weighed 17 pounds and delivered fuel economy of about 150 miles per gallon.

In July of 1945, with the war over for Italy and Turin in ruins from heavy Allied bombing in the winter of 1944, SIATA announced its plans to build the Cucciolo, which became the first new automotive design to appear in postwar Europe.

TURN AND BURN. In open air for everyone to see, the rev limit on the Gran Prix's primitive Veglia tach is marked at 13,000 rpm, an engine speed just recently reached by modern sportbike engines and not much less than the speeds at which Formula One racing engines are turned. This remarkable little engine was rated at a reliable 19 horsepower.

Because it could be clipped onto any bicycle, was reliable and got extraordinary fuel economy in a time of great economic distress, the Cucciolo was an immediate success, more so than Farinelli or his partners at SIATA anticipated. Though it eventually manufactured its own sports cars, SIATA at war's end remained a specialized engineering workshop, and by the end of 1946 demand for the Cucciolo was more than it could handle. Farinelli and SIATA began looking for a facility to manufacturer the Cucciolo.

By now the postwar Italian government had organized the Institute for Reconstruction of Industry (IRI), through which the government controlled its investments in engineering, banking, insurance, and transportation as it struggled to rebuild Italy's economic infrastructure. This was an especially daunting task, since it involved rebuilding industries destroyed by Allied bombing. Like SIATA, Ducati was precisely the sort of company IRI was formed to resuscitate.

The IRI's managers thus decided to move production of the Cucciolo to the Ducati plant in Bologna. This was a case of good news/bad news for the Ducati brothers, for the price of rebuilding was a government takeover of the facility. The brothers, with minimal takeover compensation in their pockets, emigrated to Argentina.

The IRI, meanwhile, rebuilt the bomb-shattered Ducati plant and installed the machine tools required for Cucciolo production. Thus, in 1946 Ducati became a constructor of internal-combustion engines, with Farinelli receiving a royalty on

NOT SO SEXY. The left side of the GP125 engine is notable only for the elegance of the head's casting, designed to remain rigid while its three cams and two valves worked at high temperatures and furious speeds.

each engine sold. That royalty must have amounted to a tidy sum, for 15,000 Cucciolos were sold the first year of production, with 25,000 of them sold the next year, and with an astounding 60,000 units cranked out in 1948.

By 1950 Ducati had built and sold more than 200,000 Cucciolos, and now was building the engine in several different specifications. So the company was ready for the next logical step, a complete motorcycle based on the 60-cc, 3-speed T3

Cucciolo. At first, Ducati relied upon Aero Caproni, of Trento—another IRI company—for the chassis. A year later Ducati began building the entire machine in-house, and soon after that it went racing, an action guaranteed to get the attention of the Italian public, which was as crazy for motorized competition then as today.

A Cucciolo racer and tuner named Ugo Tomarozzi was chosen as the factory's standard-bearer. In 1951 he established several new speed records, including one for 41 miles per hour for 100 miles.

By 1953 Ducati was successful enough to have established a sound economic base. It used that base to split into two separate companies, Ducati Elettronica S.p.A., still operational in Bologna not far from the Borgo Panigale factory, and Ducati Meccanica S.p.A., with Dr. Giuseppi Montano its operational chief. By 1954 Ducati Meccanica was producing 120 machines per day, and Montano took the step that would cement Ducati's identity firmly into the minds of enthusiasts. He hired Fabio Taglioni, the man whose engineering brilliance would become forever linked with Ducati's legend, to lead an engineering team capable of designing and building roadracing equipment. Taglioni and his team responded to Montano's call for an engine capable of roadracing glory by designing the 100 Gran Sport. This 98-cc engine became the progenitor of future Ducati Singles. The design was brilliantly simple, yet replete with elegant engineering solutions and graced with the technological feature that would mark Ducati engines all the way through the 1970s, into the era of the V-twins. It used an overhead camshaft driven by bevel gears and a vertical shaft drive. Additionally, the engines

SMALL, NARROW, AND LIGHT. Taglioni borrowed heavily from preceding designs for the 125 Gran Prix, so it shares the svelte profile of other early Ducati Singles, though its frame is unlike that of any of the single-cylinder streetbikes.

ALL IN THE FAMILY. A race motor it may have been, but the 125 Gran Prix clearly uses cases, clutch actuation, ignition location, shifter, exhaust sweep, and other elements that are seen in Ducati Singles all the way to the end of production.

were visually beautiful, with deep fins on the heads, cylinder barrels, and crankcases, exhibiting a general rightness of line and proportion.

The 100 Gran Sport raced with astonishing success during the 1955 season, and for 1956 was enlarged to 125 cc, a mere 7.6 cubic inches. These little engines were sturdy and very powerful, developing 16 horsepower at 11,500 rpm. But the increased rpm levels that produced that power broke valve springs or floated valves. That's how the 125 Gran Prix, a tuned, triple-overhead-cam version of the 125 Gran Sport came to be developed.

To solve the problem of broken valve springs, Taglioni eliminated them. Instead, he pressed desmodromic valve actuation, operated by three camshafts, into service. Where most engines use a camshaft lobe to open a valve and a spring to slam it closed, desmodromics calls on camshaft lobes to both push a valve open and to pull it closed. In an engine using desmodromic valve actuation, as long as the camshaft is turning as it should, the valves will open and close as they should, with engine speed, at least theoretically, playing no role in the proceedings.

Desmodromics, as a concept, was nothing new. The engines in Mercedes-Benz's 1950s Grand Prix cars were desmo units, and Mercedes capitalized on the concept with great success until it withdrew from racing in 1955, following Mercedes 300SLR driver Pierre Levegh's multiple-fatality crash into the race crowd at that year's 24 Hours of LeMans. Indeed, an Italian motorcycle manufacturer named Azzariti built machines in 1933 and 1934 that relied on desmodromic valve actuation.

Desmodromics was not in widespread use because its use required very close tolerances between parts as the desmo cylinder head was assembled. That meant it wasn't practical for production machines, but it could be very effective for

racing engines. This was a lesson Taglioni, who sketched out his first desmo engine while still an engineering student, adapted. Using a desmo head with three camshafts—one each to open the intake and exhaust valves, and a central one to close both valves—his 125 Gran Prix developed 19 horsepower at 12,500 rpm.

A 125 Gran Prix ridden by Gianni degli Antoni won its class at the 1956 Swedish Grand Prix. More Grand Prix glory seemed possible, but degli Antoni was killed during practice at the next race, the Italian GP at Monza. This moved Ducati's racing program back several steps, and Taglioni and company weren't back in earnest until 1958, when the 125-cc desmo Gran Prix dominated Italy's national racing season. The following year, Ducati concentrated most of its support on a young rider named Mike Hailwood, and the year after that, concentrated its efforts on its roadgoing motorcycles.

These were powered by the first narrowcase Single. The bike was called the 175 Sport, and it was introduced at the 1956 Milan Motorcycle Exposition. This engine featured Taglioni's design hallmarks set out in the original Gran Sport, and became the foundation of the subsequent Ducati line. That line was augmented by 100-cc and 125-cc models in 1958, a 250-cc version in 1961, and a similar 350 in 1965.

Even as Ducati struggled to increase its production of road bikes, it expanded its dealer network through Europe and as far afield as Australia, Asia, and Europe. In the United States, however, Ducati remained largely unknown. That was soon to change, thanks largely to the efforts of an enterprising pair of brothers who didn't know a lot about motorcycles, but who knew a great deal about how to sell them—so much so that they helped shape Ducati's product for decades.

TWO

THE 1960S—
SINGLES AND THE
BERLINER BROTHERS

Joseph and Michael Berliner were brothers who immigrated to the United States from their native Hungary in 1947. They both endured the Nazi terror perpetrated on residents of central Europe, but the trials of life in the camps couldn't come close to shaking from them their innate business sense. Nor could it shake from them their enthusiasm for motorcycles.

Both their business sense and their enthusiasm for motorcycles came to them early in life. With their father, the pair operated a small store in Budapest that sold radios, sewing machines, bicycles, and Zundapp motorcycles. At the end of the war there was no question of returning to Budapest and the business. Their father had been an officer in the Austro-Hungarian army during World War I, and a fervent anti-Communist. With the Soviet Union in control of Hungary following World War II, says Michael Berliner, now retired in New Jersey, "We didn't want to stay in Hungary."

TIGHT AND TINY. This gorgeous little 1961 Ducati 250 is the logical next step from the 175s that the Berliner Brothers first sold in the United States. What it had to compete against, however, was the first wave of Honda Twins. While those bikes didn't have the little Ducati's style, they had reliability, horsepower, and parts availability—all the things that Ducati owners of the day could only dream about.

BEGINNING OF A TRADITION. *Cycle World*, under editor/publisher Joe Parkhurst, developed a tradition of sponsoring race bikes. This Ducati 250 is among the very first of those. Built by *CW* staffer Gordon Jennings and ridden in 1966 at Daytona and at West Coast club races by Frank Scurria, it found itself competing against much faster Yamaha TD1Bs. Parkhurst recalls today that it held its own nicely against that fast company. *Cycle World*

So in 1947 the pair came to the United States to found the Berliner Motor Corp., with headquarters in Hasbrouck Heights, New Jersey.

Joe Berliner, the elder of the two by 17 years, started in 1948 as the American distributor of Jawa motorcycles, then, using old family connections, Zundapp, and finally Sachs machines. Following military service in Korea from 1951 through 1953, Mike Berliner joined Joe in the business to help boost sales for the growing company.

Joe Parkhurst, founding editor and publisher of *Cycle World* magazine, recalls, "Joe, with his camp tattoos, was a tough, sour old man. He was difficult to know, and he didn't speak very good English. Mike

was much younger. He was out front while Joe ran the business. They both had accents so thick it was almost comic, but they were very hard business people."

They had their work cut out for them. Americans were riding Harley-Davidsons and Indians, and were deeply in love with those large, heavy machines. Returning servicemen carried the gospel of the lightweight English motorcycles, and Triumph slowly was being discovered by American enthusiasts. But very few people had heard of Ducati. The Berliners certainly had not, not at this early point. But they knew business, and they knew motorcycles. And Mike knew how to sell.

THE BIKE TODAY. Now owned by Ducati collector Guy Webster, the former *Cycle World* racer looks better than ever. It undoubtedly would stop better than ever, thanks to updated disc brakes from a kart. They would be helpful, since this bike will run at speeds of 120 miles per hour. But they're illegal for today's vintage racing. The Ceriani fork, replacing the stock Marzocchi, is legal, though.

He loaded a pair of two-stroke Zundapps into the back of a Ford Ranchero and began driving around, visiting dealers across the United States.

Joe's sales pitches, and his faith in his dealers, worked, and the Berliner Motor Corp. was off and running. But as a distributor of motorcycles with two-stroke engines, its lines were incomplete. Berliner badly needed a motorcycle powered by a four-stroke engine. The brothers found what they needed at one of the motorcycle world's greatest institutions, the IFMA Motorcycle Exhibition, held in the fall of even-numbered years in Cologne, Germany. IFMA, or the Cologne Show, as it's known, is motorcycling's mecca. Together with Italy's EICMA International Motorcycle Exhibition (held in the fall of odd-numbered years), IFMA provides factories with a dynamic display environment that intermixes manufacturers, distributors, and consumers.

The Berliners were regular visitors to IFMA in those early years, and so was Ducati. But the company's production was so small through most of the 1950s that it was not interested in developing a United States market. Then politics intervened in the form of an agreement—perhaps, when seen in the long term, the most damaging in the company's history—between Italian unions and state-owned factories, stating that once someone was hired, he could not be laid off. Ducati's workforce grew with the postwar European motorcycle market. When that market softened, the excess workers could not be displaced. So by the late 1950s, Ducati badly needed the U.S. market.

When the Berliners went to the 1958 IFMA Show and saw Taglioni's Ducati 175 Single, they were in the right place at the right time. Berliner remembers, "The bike was just beautiful. Looking at that engine, if you were at all mechanically inclined, you looked at that overhead-cam engine, and it was just gorgeous. It had a beautiful low handlebar, low gas tank and seat—it was just out of this world. We met with Dr. Montano, the president of the company, and did a deal. We would bring in the 125 and the 175. We had a little problem at the beginning. The rocker arms were made of the same material as the cam, so they wore very fast. But the factory began making the rockers from a different material, and they worked beautiful. The rest is history."

Just as he had with Zundapp, Berliner hauled his Ducatis around to his core dealers in the back of a truck—the same dealers who had come to know and trust the Berliners and the service they gave. Ducati's newness in the marketplace, the fact that its bikes were powered by four-stroke technology, and the fact that they were beautiful, paid off. The dealers fell in love with Ducati, and so did their customers. In 1959, Ducati's first year with the Berliner brothers, the factory's goal for American sales was about 700 bikes. The Berliners sold 2,000, and in the second full year, they sold 3,000.

FLEET AND FAMOUS. By the mid-1960s Honda ruled the roost in terms of sales and success. But Ducati still owned the hearts and minds of the hard-core enthusiasts, thanks largely to this bike, the fabled Diana Mark 3. This one, is a 1965 model.

Parkhurst took a look at what the Berliners were selling, and he liked what he saw. But as interested as Parkhurst was in Berliner Motor Corp.'s products, he was even more interested in its money. He traveled to New Jersey to see if he could separate the brothers from a bit of it. He was persuasive, and the Berliners became one of *Cycle World*'s first advertisers.

The wide exposure that *Cycle World* and, later, *Cycle* provided for Ducati—not just in the paid-advertising pages, but also in the infinitely more valuable editorial pages—was precisely what Ducati and the Berliners needed. Motorcycling in the United States was still a tiny business, without the acceptance it enjoyed in Europe. Its growth required the development of good marketing tools and the growth of national enthusiast magazines to gain national awareness. Motorcycling truly was a word-of-mouth sport. Thanks to the enthusiast magazines, it didn't remain that way.

Mike Berliner remembers, "It was going up and up and up, until the big Japanese machines came in. We did so well, and it was very easy. We didn't have any competitors, and the Ducati was a motorcycle that stood by itself. To me, nothing handled like a Ducati, not even the featherbed Nortons [which, with Moto Guzzi, the Berliner Motor Corp. later distributed]. When you got on a Ducati you could get into any curve, and just by touching the tank with your knees, move the motorcycle in and out."

This kind of handling had paid off for Ducati in Europe, where the kind of racing success that great handling provided trickled down to mass appeal and therefore mass sales. It also paid off for Berliner, which by 1959 had a $2 million open account with Ducati.

More importantly, says Berliner, "We were all the best of friends with Dr. Montano, and with Ing. Taglioni."

That combination of friendship and business success gave the company tremendous influence in Italy.

Every year the Berliner Motor Corp. chartered a plane and flew 70 to 80 of its top dealers and their wives to Italy for a visit to the Ducati factory. Such trips were part pleasure, but mostly business. The meetings gave dealers a chance to suggest what might sell to their respective constituencies.

Berliner remembers telling his dealers, "I'm not smart, but I can tell you that if you like something personally, you can buy one and keep it. But to be successful, you've got to give people what they want, not necessarily what you want. As long as we make the engine and frame good and strong, the rest of the motorcycle is a facade. We've got to make sure the buyers like that facade."

So on the occasion of a dealer visit to the factory, the factory might set out 20 different fuel tanks and seats, lined up with a selection of handlebars and fenders. The dealers would come to a consensus about what combination of tank, seat, fender, and handlebar they could sell, and in what colors. And those were the tanks, seats, fenders, handlebars, and colors the American enthusiast saw when he next visited his Ducati dealer.

The Berliners' feeling that the Ducati Single was perfect for the American enthusiast of small, nimble motorcycles seemed right on the money, and in the early 1960s, there was no more influential enthusiast than Parkhurst. He remembers, "I loved the first Ducati I ever saw. It was like they were the essence of Italian motorcycling. The castings were beautiful, the finishes were nice and done in interesting colors, technically they were innovative for the time, and they were much prettier than British and American bikes."

That prettiness, Parkhurst believes, comes as a part of the Italian way of doing business. He says, "When a product shows that kind of attention, it goes well beyond being a manufacturing obligation. It's just the Italian nature. You could see it across the

REV IT UP. Tucked in behind its tiny fly screen, the Diana wears a mechanical Veglia tach. Rev limit is 8,500 rpm. The engine's uncaged-ball lower rod bearing made low engine speeds problematic, as lugging would crowd all the uncaged balls in one area of the rod's big end, leaving other areas unsupported. The design was very reliable in its mid- and upper-rpm ranges, however.

FAIR IT IN. One of the Diana's distinguishing marks was this fairing on the lower section of the tach. Usually painted, this one is chromed because the bike's owner, Guy Webster, likes it that way.

board in everything in Italy during those days. Almost everything they did was diecast. You didn't see a lot of sand castings like you did with a lot of other European bikes. That means their engineers considered the cast piece a finished product when it came out of the mold. This was really important, because not only did such castings have a certain polished beauty, but more importantly, the cases fit together properly and they didn't leak. The care

their engineers showed, their attention to detail, all reflected fine engineering principles.

"I'll never forget, the first Ducati we ever tested was a Diana. Boy, I loved that bike. It ran like gang-busters, looked neat with that big Dell 'Orto carb sticking out of the cylinder head—Ducati, to me, just exemplified the very best in Italian engineering, style, and design. I bought that Diana. I couldn't resist it. It was really pretty and ran so good—it

ITALIAN ELECTRICS. The Diana had a weird Achilles' heel in that when its taillight bulb shorted out, the entire system would die as a result of that short. The Italian-engineering solution? A switch to kill power to the taillight, neatly circumventing, though not solving, the problem.

turned nearly 10,000 rpm. It was smooth, so much fun to ride, so much fun to listen to, that's when I really got hooked on Ducati. I later put the engine into a Metisse chassis, and Bob Atkinson, who became editor of *Cycle World*, still has it."

Phil Schilling, who as a staff editor would build the Ducati 750 Super Sport that *Cycle* editor-in-chief Cook Neilson rode to a win in the 1977 Daytona Superbike race, was another enthusiast who became

involved with Ducatis almost as soon as the Berliners began bringing them to the U.S.

Schilling remembers, "I sent off a letter to Berliner Motor Corp. and got all these brochures and stuff back. Boy, these things really looked neat. The engines were startling and weird. They didn't look right. Now people say the Ducati Single is one of most beautiful engines ever done, but that's not what people thought early on. Here was an engine so strange, so over the top, that you really had to understand the engineering logic behind it. To guys like me, they were really appealing because they had gear-driven overhead cams.

"Here I was, a guy with no engineering background, but I knew all the buzz words, and I knew overhead cams were good. Then I found out that Ducati had these very fancy triple-cam desmodromics in its racebikes. I thought these must be the chariots of the gods. In 1954 and 1955, Mercedes-Benz had run desmo valves. I'd really followed grand prix racing in those years; when this magic word 'desmodromic' popped up again, they had me."

Ducati and Berliner acquired other enthusiasts as well, but it was almost too late, for a revolution in the way the motorcycle business was conducted was under way. This was just at the time when Honda proved that a clever advertising slogan like, "You meet the nicest people on a Honda," could be tremendously effective. By comparison, the advertising for most of the European motorcycle brands was, even by the standards of the 1960s, parochial and poorly done.

The Japanese were changing the face of the motorcycle business in another way. The Japanese factories all maintained large engineering staffs that allowed them to produce an ever-widening stream of new products and model lines with relatively short production lives. Ducati's engineering department, in contrast, was composed of a small team that was not given the budget to develop an ongoing line of products. This meant that compared to the ever-evolving technologies of the Japanese, Ducati's technology

CLUB RACER. If you were a racer in the 1960s and determined to ignore the obvious superiority of Yamaha's TD1 in its A, B, and C versions, this is what you might have raced. If, that is, you were lucky enough to have had access to noted restorer Todd Millar, who built this example. These little Ducati Single racers were light and nimble, with adequate brakes. They were, however, unable to compete with the Yamahas, which were fragile but very fast.

was in danger of becoming stale. Suddenly, one of Ducati's great strengths, its reliance on the elegance and longevity of its single-cylinder engine design, became a weakness.

Indeed, the engineering methodology followed by most European factories involved building on existing designs; offering a well-proven engine, transmission, and chassis combination over a long period of time; changing a motorcycle's bodywork at occasional intervals to help stimulate new model sales; and changing the engine/transmission/chassis only when absolutely necessary. Companies like Ducati, feeding a traditional and stable European

market, had neither the engineering staff nor the mindset to react quickly to changing trends. This was exactly opposite the model proliferation embraced by the Japanese as they pursued a volatile and growing American market.

Ducati's loyalty to its engine and transmission designs should have meant a ready supply of spare parts, but this was one of the battles the Berliners fought repeatedly with the factory. The Berliners insisted on maintaining a large and complete parts department. From the factory's point of view, however, supplying the Berliners with spares just was not economical, for it could make far more money if it sold the parts assembled as complete motorcycles, not as individual items. These divergent points of view continue to haunt Ducati, and to make life difficult for its customers, as the scarcity of spares remains a fact of life for many Ducati dealers.

One of the elements that helped ensure Ducati's survival in the face of increasing Japanese competitiveness was that the Berliner brothers had large amounts of hard cash. They were willing to use it to front the developments they thought Ducati needed

STATE OF TUNE. This detail of a Ducati 250-cc race engine illustrates the elegance of the mechanical cam drive, taken from the cam-drive bevel gears. The chromed header pipe seen here empties into a flat-black, reverse megaphone, very much 1960s-style.

to continue to be competitive in the American marketplace. The factory needed the money.

Mike Berliner remembers, "The factory always was underfunded. There never was enough money to develop new models. In the early days the Italian government had to subsidize the factory because it never made enough money to carry itself. I mean, the factory had at least 150 employees it couldn't lay off. And it couldn't increase the prices of its motorcycles, because if it did that, it wouldn't be competitive. So when the factory's managers would ask for more money from IRI, which had its headquarters in Rome, the IRI managers would complain that the factory was costing the government too much money. They'd say, 'Look, we're thinking about giving the factory to somebody else and letting them make spark plugs.' They [the IRI] didn't want to make money. They wanted to take care of the workers."

The Japanese manufacturers, meanwhile, were making headway with extremely competitive products. That meant that enthusiast racers, like Schilling, who insisted on sticking with their beloved Ducati Diana 250s, were in trouble. By now Yamaha was selling the TD1B and TD1C, powerful two-stroke racebikes, much faster than the Ducati Singles they competed against.

Yamaha's racing strength appeared to weaken when Taglioni finally was able to put a desmo head into production. In 1968, Ducati introduced a revised Single featuring strengthened internals and crankcases with wider-spaced rear engine mounts. The first bike to feature this new "widecase" engine was a spring-valve 350 street-scrambler, which appeared at the Cologne show in 1967. This was followed in 1968 by the 250-cc and 350-cc Mark 3 Desmos, the first desmodromic streetbikes.

"I thought, hmm, a desmo 250. These guys may be back. This could be the big Ducati breakthrough; maybe now we'll be able to do battle with the really good Yamahas," remembers Schilling.

But no. Though these new widecase engines featured desmodromic valve actuation, they failed to

TIME WARP. This 1965 Sebring 350, owned and raced by the author in AHRMA vintage events, is not that different from similar bikes that raced in the 1960s. One important difference is that modern tires are far superior to those raced upon when this bike was new. Characteristic of these solid little machines, all that's required between races is clean oil and a valve adjustment.

make substantially more horsepower than the Dianas of the early 1960s because the Ducati combustion chamber design was inefficient. Though Taglioni had managed to transplant his desmodromic technology to production equipment, in doing so he failed to make any substantive changes to the head and combustion chamber, which featured a highly domed piston and valves set at a very large included angle. This precluded effective cylinder-filling, as the air/fuel charge rushing in through the inlet port was partially blocked by the piston's dome at the top part of the intake stroke. So lacking the narrower included valve angle and flatter-topped pistons of modern engines, the new desmo engines could turn to higher rpm levels than their valve-spring counterparts, but to very little practical effect. Additionally, though the engines were sturdy, the widecase bikes were up to 20 pounds heavier than the narrowcase bikes they replaced.

Ducati wasn't staying current, and it paid the price. Through the marque's early years in the United States, partly because of support of the enthusiast magazines, Ducatis had a chance to become almost-mainstream motorcycles. As the 1960s progressed into the following decade, and the manufacturing and engineering strength and marketing clout of the Japanese manufacturers grew, Ducati's chance disappeared, and it became marginalized as a brand.

Cycle World's Parkhurst opines, "Through the 1960s awareness of Ducati remained fairly light. The market here was unsophisticated, and didn't really develop the kind of sophisticated taste and desire for bikes like the Ducati. I think the Berliners were determined to build Ducati into something. But I think they couldn't have cared less in Italy."

In Japan, however, the manufacturers cared very much indeed. As a result, the American motorcycle market got a huge nudge in the direction of sophistication from Honda, in the form of, first, the 250-cc Hawk and, later, the 305-cc Super Hawk. A customer could buy a Ducati Single, which even with its desmo head still offered what was, essentially, 1950s kick-start technology. Or, for about the same money, the customer could buy a state-of-the-art, electric-start Twin that offered absolutely stunning performance for its size, and even better reliability. The choice was, for most enthusiasts, an easy one. They bought the Honda Super Hawk and started Honda down the road toward the supremacy it now enjoys.

What kept Ducati alive during these times was a core of enthusiasts who remained true to their weird Italian Singles.

Recalls Schilling, "There was a certain elitism at work here. Anybody could go buy a Super Hawk. But the Ducati was a kind of special, marginal, niche bike. The interesting thing was all of those people I knew who had that point of view liked goofy bikes."

Ducati, meanwhile, just kept pushing along with what it had. That wasn't enough, and Taglioni knew it. For by 1968, a 350-cc desmo Ducati, which really displaced just 340 cc, had to compete against not just Honda's potent 305-cc Super Hawk, which appeared in 1961 to almost immediate acceptance, but the Honda CB/CL350, which also appeared in 1968. This was the next giant step beyond the Super Hawk, and as fine a piece of equipment as the Super Hawk was, the CB/CL350 was even better. Competing against these Hondas was a hopeless task, and the Berliners and the Italians watched helplessly as Honda sales pushed into the stratosphere—in 1965, with 20,000 Super Hawk 305s sold, and in 1972 with 131,000 CB/CL350s sold.

And Honda wasn't the only company pushing the performance and sales envelopes. Yamaha was right there battling for its share of the market, and so were other Japanese manufacturers. Even the Italians now knew something had to be done.

THREE

THE 1970s—
V-TWINS AND
JAPANESE DOMINANCE

During the 1960s most of the American motorcycle-buying pool was composed of first-time buyers. By the beginning of the 1970s, a fundamental shift had occurred. Now just a small percentage of buyers were first-timers. The rest already owned motorcycles, and were looking to move up to bigger, faster machines—bikes such as Honda's revolutionary CB750, introduced in 1969. Clearly, Ducati was in trouble, with nothing on the horizon that could compete with the multicylinder wonders from Japan.

Ducati chief engineer Fabio Taglioni was ready with just what this market needed in the way of a revolutionary new engine. Ducati itself, always underfunded and suspecting that the buoyancy of the American motorcycle market was a temporary anomaly, wasn't. As early as 1962 Taglioni possessed finished drawings for a 750-cc V-twin. Such a configuration was a natural, for as Taglioni envisioned this engine, it wasn't much more complicated than two sets of Ducati Single cylinders and heads mounted on an all-new crankcase.

CAN IT. The chromed shrouds around the 450 Desmo's instruments were known to enthusiasts of the day as "coffee cans." Note that the instruments mount directly to the top of the Marzocchi fork legs which extend through the top of the upper triple clamp.

AN EXCUSE? OR A REASON? This 450 Desmo proudly wears a period "Made in Italy" decal just aft of its fuel filler. For many enthusiasts, that's reason enough to own such a quirky machine.

STYLE OVER SPEED. The 1972 450 Desmo widecase is a study in Italian style. This one, owned by Guy Webster, has been modified to make it more usable as a daily-driver. It uses a 29-mm flat-slide carb; a Conti silencer, in place of the stock Silentium, and a front twin-leading shoe brake that uses an enlarged cooling scoop.

But in 1962 Ducati's Singles were selling nicely, and despite the American enthusiast's historic relationship with large-capacity V-twin motorcycles, the Italians refused to believe a market for such a bike existed. In this refusal to press forward, the corporate cultures of Ducati, one of the traditionalist Europeans, and Honda, a representative of the new-wave Japanese, could not have been more different. Honda was then, and is now, committed to the constant development of new products.

By the very late 1960s it was abundantly clear, even to Ducati's government bosses in Rome, that time was wasting. Because of Taglioni's earlier work, once he finally received the go-ahead to produce a 750-cc V-twin, tooling could be ordered and production cranked up fairly quickly. The result was the 750GT, introduced in 1971.

"We flipped right away for it—it was just gorgeous," says Berliner. "We really needed it to get the factory moving. The V-twin was a breakthrough. Ducati wouldn't have survived with its small machines; the competition was very strong."

But Ducati had waited too long with the V-twin and lost its fragile momentum in the United States,

DIRT DEVIL. An oddity by any definition, that was the Ducati RT450. Sold in the United States only in 1971, it had no more power than a 350 in spite of its desmo design yet, thanks to a very sturdy and rigid frame, was considerably heavier than any 350. In Europe, the bike was known as the TSS and was intended to compete against the BSA Victor. *Jim Miller*

and many of its customers. Yet even in the relatively small numbers in which it was available, the bike was a success in more ways than one.

Mike Berliner, who continued to make the rounds of his dealers, found that the V-Twin was easy to sell. He'd stop at a dealership, unload a bike and invite the dealer to take a ride. Invariably, he recalls, the dealers would come back from those rides and ask how quickly they could get a supply of the bikes.

Berliner says, "The V-twin's handling and its looks sold it. Americans are wonderful people in this regard. If something catches their eye, if they like it, they'll buy it. The Germans might be interested in something, but they'd look at the

blueprints, check the clearances, and see how everything wears. They're pretty technically minded. In America if it looks and rides good they don't care what's going to happen tomorrow, they want it right now."

Cycle World's Parkhurst says, "I loved that first V-twin. Its performance was only fair, but Ducati seemed on its way again."

The company was on its way again in large measure not just because it had a large-capacity bike, but because the 750 V-twin worked a lot better compared to its competition than even the largest Ducati Single had ever done. Honda's introduction of the CB750 in 1969 established the transverse four-cylinder

GLIMMER KING. This detail shot shows the coarse nature of the metallic flakes used in this bike's paint. Paint with very fine flakes was difficult to apply with period spray-painting equipment, so large flakes were the obvious choice for any production stylist intent on applying metalflake to his creation.

FLAKY. Italian style isn't a surefire thing, as this 1973 350 Desmo Silver Shotgun proves. Sure, its line and proportion are both exemplary, and so is its 350-cc Desmo widecase engine. But silver metalflake paint? By this time—the widecase Desmos appeared in 1968—the influence of American buyers was being felt by the Ducati factory.

TOO LITTLE, TOO LATE. Ducati attempted to shore up its sagging fortunes with a machine powered by a vertical Twin, first of 350 cc and eventually of 500 cc. The bike was an unmitigated disaster, with poor styling and performance. This bike, a 500 GTL, was built in 1977. It's exhaust system is nonstock.

EYE OF THE BEHOLDER. A close look at the 500 GTL engine reveals it as a blocky, heavy-looking contraption. Though reliable and oil-tight, it was rejected by enthusiasts.

engine as the motorcycling world's orthodox power-plant. The orthodoxy also included a certain amount of overengineering, which meant Japanese bikes tended to be heavier than perhaps they absolutely needed to be. And it meant that as superb as these engines may have been, often the chassis that carried them didn't match up.

By now Parkhurst's *Cycle World* had been joined as a magazine of tremendous influence by *Cycle*, which under editor Cook Neilson and eventual editor Phil Schilling became highly respected for both technical and literary excellence. With more than a half-million copies sold each month, *Cycle* was big enough to have tremendous clout.

So when Neilson and Schilling decided to include a Ducati 750GT in a big-bike comparison test in December 1973, enthusiasts—those who were predisposed to alternative motorcycles and those who were not—had to be interested.

Neilson and Schilling were interested because Mike Berliner's marketing efforts had extended to them, and were successful. By now the 750GT had been on sale in Europe for about a year, and Berliner needed to be sure the bike was suitable for the United States. So he brought several of them over and invited Neilson and Schilling to ride two of them. The pair rode the bikes on the street and flogged them around Bridgehampton Raceway in Connecticut. They were impressed, and the Ducati V-twin went into *Cycle's* next comparison test.

Recalls Schilling, "I think that comparison test probably provided the rationale for the 750 in this country. What *Cycle* said was, 'This motorcycle really makes sense, not just on its own terms, but in terms of comparison with others.'"

The competition, Schilling recalls, was fearsome. Kawasaki's Z-1 had just been introduced, and it was the latest and best example of the Japanese four-cylinder motorcycle. It won the comparison test. But *Cycle's* editors were so impressed with the Ducati 750GT that three of them bought Ducatis. The magazine's comparison, and the actions of its editors, who would write extensively about their Ducatis, endorsed the Ducati V-twin as something a motorcycle enthusiast could legitimately buy and enjoy, despite its always marginal electronics and uneven paint quality.

Neilson and Schilling were convinced that the Ducati 750GT's strengths outweighed its weak-

ONE BECOMES TWO. It's possible to say that this 1974 750 Sport represents a certain unwillingness to deal with reality. By now the Japanese were building very fast, very reliable four-cylinder motorcycles, and they were selling every one they could ship to the United States. Ducati, meanwhile, seized on the notion of combining two of its single-cylinder engines on a common crankshaft. This bike, now a cult classic, was the result.

THE BEGINNING AND THE END. Ducati's Singles and its V-twins overlapped in 1974, the final year of Single production and the first year for the V-twins. This pair illustrates how closely related the bikes—both from the design studio of Fabio Taglioni—were.

nesses. Neilson says, "The appeal seemed absolutely obvious. These bikes had an absolutely unique sound. It wasn't that it was loud, it was that it was so distinct you could hear it for miles. And that engine configuration led to a really pleasant smoothness. It had terrific power and torque, and the bike was relatively light, so it stopped and handled well."

Neilson was so impressed with the 750GT that he decided to go racing on it, with Schilling, the

END OF THE LINE. This 1974 Ducati 350 Desmo represents, finally, a change of thinking at Ducati's Bologna factory. Though Taglioni had been drawing V-twins for several years, his bosses were unwilling to spend the money to build them. Finally they were forced to make the change, and this model, with its disc front brake, was the final widecase Single built by Ducati.

LESS IS MORE. It took American enthusiasts a while to figure it out, but the Italians were onto something. The 750 Sport was light and rigid and offered lots of torque and a favorable power-to-weight ratio. But by 1974 when the bike debuted, it was almost too little, too late.

hard-headed Ducati enthusiast, as his tuner. And he wrote about his experiences, extensively and eloquently, in a series called "Beyond Racer Road." These appearances in *Cycle* resulted in the kind of publicity Ducati never could have purchased, for this kind of publicity never is for sale.

The 750GT was well adapted to duty as a racing mount, with its rigid frame and modest but tractable horsepower. Its steering was slow, in comparison to that of the Japanese bikes, but the V-twin's overall stability and the user-friendliness of its engine's power delivery inspired, as Ducatis still do today, a tremendous amount of rider confidence.

Says Schilling, "Having a motorcycle that really inspires confidence in you as a rider allows you to believe that you can do this. You believe this when the equipment works right, and stuff isn't happening that you don't understand."

Taglioni, who at this writing is comfortably retired and looking after his garden of exotic succulents, remained convinced that the V-twin Ducati still could benefit from increased performance. So he finalized the design for two 750GT variants—the 750 Sport, introduced in late 1972, and desmodromic 750 Super Sport. To help boost 750 sales, Ducati factory brass decided to build 10 of the desmo bikes for the purpose of racing in 1972's inaugural Imola 200, with British rider Paul Smart nominated to ride one of them. To all-around amazement, Smart won this race, helping Ducati sales in Europe and catching the attention of enthusiasts everywhere.

Americans never have been strong roadracing enthusiasts, and so probably weren't influenced as heavily by Smart's Imola 200 victory as were European enthusiasts. But they were influenced enough

ICON. The most collectable, most desirable vintage Ducati? It's probably this bike—a 1973 750 Super Sport. The Super Sport designation comes from the engine's advanced state of tune and from its use of desmodromic valve actuation. Painted silver and blue, these bikes changed hue over time as the varnish sprayed over the color coat yellowed.

SEX SELLS. Can you say, "Sixties?" The Berliners selected an ad layout clearly imprinted with the look of the 1960s to promote the spring-head 750. Then, she was racy. Now the bike seems more so. *Zack Miller Collection*

to take notice of the 750 Sport, which offered a more sporting seating position than the 750GT, along with higher compression and bigger carburetors. But that wasn't the end of the line, for the 750 Sports still had valve-spring heads. Ducati raised the ante at 1973's Milan Motorcycle Exhibition by debuting the 750 Super Sport, which with its desmodromic valve system was a street-legal replica of the Imola racebike.

Schilling remembers, "In April 1972 I went to Imola and saw the Ducatis win the first Imola 200, and I spent most of the week at the factory watching the team get ready. So here, finally, is the desmo

principle that seems to work. Those bikes were pretty terrific bikes. They were essentially production bikes with desmo heads. This group of 10 racebikes were the precursors to the 750SS, though they'd been prepped with slightly fiercer cams than the 750SS. The factory people told me they were thinking about doing a street replica of the Imola racebikes. And I said that if they did that, I wanted one. One was sent to me at *Cycle*, and then two other *Cycle* editors bought them. And that's how the first three 750 Super Sports came to the United States."

Because of Neilson's racing program, Schilling said, it seemed obvious to him that the first of the

Super Sports to arrive ought to be dedicated to him. That bike became the famed *California Hot Rod*, also known as "Old Blue", the 750SS that won the Daytona Superbike race at Daytona in 1977 with Neilson aboard. The bike originally intended for Neilson thus went to Schilling, who still owns it.

Neilson, now far removed from motorcycles and magazines, says of the Ducatis, "There was something special, something different about them. It was hard to put your finger on it. With the Ducati mystique comes the acceptance of certain kinds of flaws, a willingness to put up with certain character traits that you wouldn't put up with from a piece of equipment that came from a different part of the world.

"For instance, the first 750 Super Sport we ever got had a fly cast into the fuel tank. The Italians had laid up this fiberglass tank and this critter got trapped in there. That's all part of the deal. Certain things were not exactly first rate. The chassis finish not that great, the electrical systems were ratty and unfinished—it's the same kinds of things the Harley guys put up with. It's just a different set of expectations. Now, somewhere, that fuel tank still exists. We made a fuss about it over the years. I hope somebody sands 'em all down and finds it."

Neilson and Schilling, while producing *Cycle* magazine during the day, spent their off hours not worrying about that fly, but racing, tuning, rebuilding, racing, tuning, and racing. They raced "Old Blue" through 1974, 1975, 1976, and 1977, the year Neilson won at Daytona, easily the marque's most prestigious win in the United States to that point. In doing so, and in writing about their exploits, the pair cemented another block into Ducati's cult-like reputation.

Years later, commenting on that reputation, Neilson, ever the practical racer, said, "The reason we latched onto a Ducati to race had nothing to do with the fact that it was Italian and oddball. It was because we took a look at it and thought, dog-gone it, we could really do some good with this. From a practical, hard-eyed view, we figured we could take

this bike, soup it up, and beat fours with it. It was a terrific challenge.

"Its not like what it provided was something that was intangible, apparent only to people who loved Italian motorcycles. Ducatis performed, better in many ways than anything else. They were light and they handled absolutely great. They didn't make as much power as the Japanese fours, but it was easier to deal with a slight power deficiency than it was to deal with a bike that didn't handle properly. If you get a bike you can trust, you can do a lot of business with it. So, it's not like there's this myth that made the bikes desirable. There was nothing mythic about it. It was very real."

And yet Ducati's overall status in America's enthusiast community today is nothing if not mythic. Asked if *Cycle*'s influence played a role in developing that myth, Neilson said, "That's impossible to answer. I suspect that the fact that we as a group clearly adored Ducati V-twins had some effect. I suspect that the fact we had some success racing them had some effect, that we continually tested them and raced them and wrote about them probably had some effect. This was a time when *Cycle* had a monthly circulation of 520,000 readers. So among those readers, they sensed that this was something we believed in and supported. We were sincere in our affection for Ducati. We rode everything there was, and we never rode anything better than that."

Or, as Neilson wrote in the January 1976 issue of *Cycle*, "The Super Sport [is] the most functionally superior motorcycle that has ever been produced for public consumption."

High praise indeed, the sort of affirmation that no amount of advertising dollars ever can buy. Yet Ducati remained largely unable to capitalize on all the positive press it received in the United States. Schilling says, with what must be considerable understatement, "I'm not sure Ducati had enough product at the time to take advantage of this. Fewer than 100 of these bikes (the 750SS) ever were brought into the country, and all of them would have been sold with-

BIG, FAST, LOUD. This is a 1975 Ducati 900SS Imola. Though standard 900SS bikes were built by the hundreds from 1975 to 1982, just 40 highly-tuned Imola versions were built. The 900SS in its limited-production Imola form was so successful that standard 900-cc models were put into the 1976 model line.

out Neilson ever doing anything. They would have gone to people like me who would see them as the ultimate expression of this kind of bike.

"But the fact that people started to follow the [the Racer Road] series in *Cycle* certainly helped Ducati to some unknown degree. I've got to believe that there was a positive outcome for Ducati. People still were talking about "Old Blue" years after Neilson left the magazine. People remember the *California Hot Rod.*"

Did that institutionalized enthusiast memory help Ducati handle the bumps that existed through the marque's lean times in the 1980s? Schilling says now, "It had to help. Especially if you were a Ducati enthusiast, if you'd bought one of these bikes, it gave you something to go back and read. It verified that you made the right choices. If you were a Ducati enthusiast, you always knew about Daytona 1977, and you also knew about Mike Hailwood and his comeback win at the Isle of Man. What Hailwood did was just mind-boggling."

Hailwood was, of course, a multi-time world roadracing champion who gave up motorcycles to go racing cars in Formula One. He retired following a crash in his McLaren-Ford M-23 at the 1974 German Grand Prix at the Nürburgring in which his right leg was broken in three places. He was lured back to motorcycles in 1978 for a one-time crack at the Isle of Man aboard a specially prepared 900SS. Hailwood, for all his prodigious talent, shouldn't have won. But he did. And that victory became another element of the Ducati legend in the United States and Europe.

The 900SS was an enlarged member of the 750GT's spawn, a spawn that originated, oddly enough, in Australia, according to Mike Berliner. He remembers that a distributor Down Under bored out the cylinders and put in larger pistons to reach 860 cc.

As Berliner remember it, "He showed it to Taglioni. And Taglioni said, 'I don't want to make that. It will vibrate too much. I will design my own, so that I can rebalance the crank.' Six months later I went to Bologna and there at a track test was the

RACER. This detail shot reveals the 900 Imola's voluptuous tank and the spare nature of its fitments. Then, as now, Ducatis were racebikes that evolved into streetbikes.

THE VIEW. This is, undoubtedly, the way most non-Ducati-mounted riders saw these 900SS Imolas in their day. Note the narrowness of that rear tire, which had to cope with what must have been up to 70 horsepower.

44

FOR A LEGEND. They called him Mike the Bike, this hero named Mike Hailwood. Long before he returned from Formula One cars to vanquish all comers at the Isle of Man, Hailwood earned his racing stripes aboard tiny Ducati Singles. Because of the immense popularity of Hailwood's island victory, Ducati built a series of these Mike Hailwood Replicas.

900. The 900SS came out of that because Taglioni wanted something special, something lighter."

As a result of Taglioni's persistent desire for excellence, the 900SS was introduced in 1975. But even Taglioni couldn't avoid the 860.

Few people had a clearer understanding of the 860, built while the 900 was being finalized, than Mike Berliner. He recalls, "The 860 just wasn't as smooth [as the 750] and was not as acceptable to riders. It was the vibration problem that Taglioni talked about. But it was just an interim model. Later, when the 900SS came in 1975 [to be followed by the 900-cc Darmahs], that was perfect."

The Darmah was followed, in 1984, by the 900S2s, by a few 1000S2s, and by even fewer Mike Hailwood Replicas—900-cc celebrations of Hailwood's Isle of Man victory produced between 1978 and 1986. But even while it was building these bikes, Ducati very nearly disappeared.

The flattening of Ducati's business wasn't because Taglioni was out of ideas. Indeed, he'd been working on drawings of a compact V-four. But this proceeded no further than drawings. Taglioni actually built a V-four, but it was much less elegant than the one he'd originally proposed. This one was an 80-horsepower, 1,260-cc contraption called the Apollo. It was done as a prototype police motorcycle for the Berliners, who were looking to attract police business away from Harley-Davidson. It might actually have reached production. But as usual, Ducati had no money to institute development and production.

Once again, Ducati was facing stiff competition from the Japanese, who by now were building sophis-

WHAT'S IT LIKE OUT THERE? It's March 1977, Daytona International Speedway. Cook Neilson is aboard the *California Hot Rod*, the 750SS that might be the most famous Ducati of them all, coping with abundant prerace butterflies. Tuner Phil Schilling, a reporter's tape machine stuck into his face, is answering questions. *Tom Riles*

YES! The *California Hot Rod*, or "Old Blue," as the *Cycle* magazine duo called it, has done it. It's not only outlasted Daytona, it's beat all comers. Elation was the order of the day. *Tom Riles*

ticated four-valve fours. Ducati had nothing with which to do battle except an air-cooled, carbureted, two-valve V-twin. And the company already had sold about as many of those as it could reasonably expect to. For as Schilling wonders, "If you bought a 900SS in 1977, what reason would you have to buy another Ducati two or three years down the road? So I'm not really surprised that Ducati found itself headed toward stagnation or tragedy. That was its pattern."

This was a pattern that troubled the Berliners deeply. While the Japanese were selling motorcycles in huge numbers, Berliner Motor Corp.'s sales of Ducati motorcycles peaked during the mid-1970s at about 7,000 units, but even then the trend was obvious. The Berliners tried to alter the pattern in 1976.

Mike Berliner recounts, "Ducati was going downhill because the top people in Rome didn't allow the company to make changes. This was a government-owned company, remember, and anything that got done, the government had to approve, whether it was new machinery for the factory or new designs. They didn't want to approve production of the V-four. My brother offered to contribute $400,000 to the cost of the tooling. He said he'd write them a check, but they'd have to agree that this loan would be deducted from the prices of the motorcycles we bought. They wouldn't do that. They wanted to have it both ways."

So the Berliners decided to take matters into their own hands. Says Mike Berliner, "In 1976 we went to Rome and made an offer to buy Ducati. The government people there who managed the factory said that they were ready to sell, and on our terms. The reason the sale didn't go through was not a money situation. The problem was that they told us we couldn't let any of Ducati's people go, that all the people employed by Ducati as of that day would have to remain."

The Berliners, always ready to deal, proposed an alternative. They would hire a top American manager to run Ducati. They proposed that after two months, that manager would analyze the work force and its methods. He'd have the authority to hire and

OLD FRIENDS. It's March at Daytona, 20 years after Phil Schilling, Cook Neilson, and a modified 750SS known as "Old Blue" or the *California Hot Rod* scored a historic victory. Schilling and Neilson are little changed. Even less changed is the *California Hot Rod*, back for a celebration of its Daytona victory. *Tom Riles*

UNCHANGED MELODY. "Sounds like. . . ." Well, sounds like Cook and "Old Blue." The pair makes a lap, Neilson still using his distinctive riding style and, after all these years, still fitting quite nicely into his old leathers. *Tom Riles*

maintain productive members of the workforce, and to eliminate the deadwood.

Berliner recalls, "They went away and met for four days and then said 'no' to our deal. They said because of the power of the unions in Italy, the government just couldn't afford to make the deal our way. So nothing happened. We tried also to buy the Moto Guzzi factory, with similar results. This was the biggest problem in Italy."

So, but for the power of Italian unions and the inability and/or unwillingness of Italy's politicians and bureaucrats to buck that power, Ducati might have come under American ownership a full 20 years before the Texas Pacific Group managed to secure half the company in 1996.

By now the Berliners knew they were seeing the beginning of the end of their involvement with Ducati. Ironically, the problem that forced them to close the Berliner Motor Corporation stemmed only in part from the Italians. More of it stemmed from the high quality of the Japanese products, the effectiveness of the marketing programs for those products, and from certain Japanese business practices.

The Berliners believed the Japanese motorcycle manufacturers were dumping their products—that is, they were selling motorcycles in the U.S. for less than the same products sold for in Japan. The fact that Ducati's managers had made a disastrous decision to replace the company's dated but well-respected Singles with a pair of 350-cc and 500-cc vertical twins, sold from 1975 through 1983, was almost the last straw. These bikes, avail-

A RETHINK. In more ways than one the Pantah (this one, from the Guy Webster collection, was sold new in the United States as a 1979 model) represented a move into modern production for Ducati. It was smooth and quiet; it used an electric starter, and most important, the engine, with its cams driven by Gilmer belts instead of by vertical geared shafts, was far less labor-intensive to build than the old bevel-drive twins.

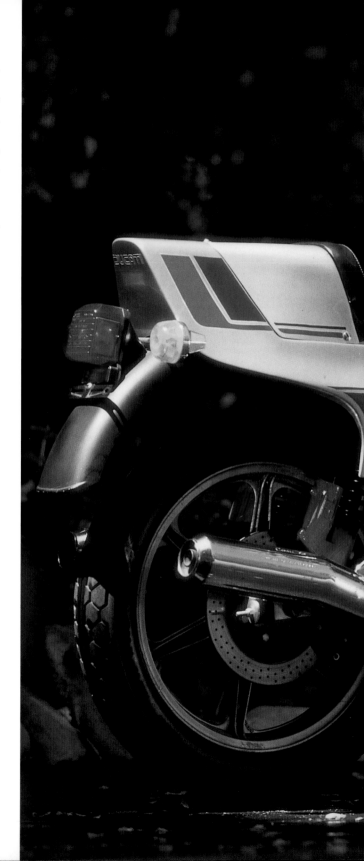

FINAL REFINEMENT. The Darmah 900SS was a development of two machines: the Darmah SD and the 900SS. It represented the best of both worlds in that it was faster and more handsome than the SD and much more refined than the sharply honed 900SS. It was built only during 1979 and 1980 and thus constituted a last gasp for Taglioni's beloved bevel-drive V-twin. This bike is from the Guy Webster collection.

STUDIO STYLE. Ducati, under the leadership of the Berliner Brothers, kicked off American awareness of the 900SS, Ducati's newest secret weapon, with this ad photo. Note that the bike's considerable wheelbase and its generous rake and trail, evidenced by the amount of space between the front wheel and the forward cylinder, accentuate the huge chassis differences between sportbikes in the 1970s and those just 25 years further along. *Zack Miller Collection*

able with either valve-spring (GTL) or desmo (GTV) heads, were contrived because of the success Honda and Yamaha enjoyed with their own vertical twins, in an American market that had grown to love British vertical twins.

Unfortunately, when it came up with these two unloved machines, Ducati was deserted by its usual design and styling expertise. At their 1975 debut the bikes not only were clumsy looking, they also vibrated, and didn't work very well. They didn't seem to carry the Ducati family genetics.

Joe Parkhurst remembers, "The bike could have made it anywhere. It didn't look Italian. They weren't trim and elegant like the British vertical twins. So this attempt to get into a U.S. bike market, which at that point was about 400,000 units a year, was quite unsuccessful."

Taglioni couldn't have been terribly surprised at the failure of the vertical twins to generate a positive response. For while the factory tried to iron the bugs out of the GTL/GTV, he was working on his next V-twin, which became known as the Pantah. This, which started life as a 500-cc unit, used Taglioni's beloved desmodromics. Like his other V-engines, it was configured with 90 degrees between the two cylinders to take advantage of the perfect primary balance of such a layout.

Schilling points out, "The bevel-drive engine was very labor intensive when it came to production. The factory was building stuff the old way, because labor was cheap. The old bevel-drive engines have got so many shims in them . . . you do lots of shims

because you can't make the product to tight-enough tolerances in the first place because the design doesn't lend itself to that. So in the bevel-drive V-twin, you have this wonderful contrivance that, really, to build it is a labor of love to get it just right. They didn't get around to building smarter until later."

Where the old bevel-drive V-twin was difficult and expensive to assemble, the Pantah was far more modern, and was designed for easy mass production. It abandoned the bevel cam drive and its elegant external shaft tower for a system that incorporated toothed pulleys and Gilmer belts, the system employed on today's Ducatis. It was indeed built smarter.

But not smart enough. For while Taglioni's last great engine design was a winner, an extension of his original desmodromic design that has carried Ducati all the way into the 1990s, the way it was approached represented another of Ducati's lost opportunities.

The problem with the Pantah was neither the engine itself nor the Pantah SL and TL motorcycles, for all their clumsy styling. Rather, the problem was that in a world dominated by large-capacity Japanese fours, Ducati introduced this all-new V-twin as a 500. It slowly enlarged the engine to 600 cc, to 650 cc, and finally to 750, but this was too little, too late. Ducati needed a logical successor to its 750-cc bevel-drive V-twin. That successor finally came along in the form of the 750-cc F1, a no-frills, sharply drawn sportbike—which is what the Pantah should have been in the first place. But the F1 wasn't released until 1985.

Ducati's inability to field a new, upgraded 750 came at the worst possible time, for fate and business reality were closing in. And though the company limped on, building a few bikes a year, eventually it was swamped by a Japanese tide.

The Berliners, whose distribution contract with the factory ran through 1995, were convinced that the Japanese were pursuing unfair business practices. They tried to do something about it.

Mike Berliner says, "We hired a couple of attorneys and went to Washington to ask President Jimmy Carter to do something about the dumping. He assigned Mr. Robert Strauss [a White House troubleshooter and one-time head of the Democratic Party] to look into it, and I got a letter from [Strauss] saying he'd do everything he could do to stop it. In the meantime I asked Harley-Davidson to intervene. They were only interested after President Carter left office. Then, finally they asked the government to put a quota on large-capacity machines."

But by that time the economic pressures on Berliner Motor Corp.—and therefore on Ducati in America—were too great to withstand. While Ducati's Twins were not as hopelessly mired in the past as the designs of some of the British motorcycle manufacturers who also went bankrupt during this period, they faced some of the same pressures that eventually caused the British manufacturers—BSA, Norton, Triumph, and the rest—into bankruptcy. These pressures resulted from the awesome might of Japan, Inc., which was selling beautifully engineered and produced equipment in the United States, and selling it for prices the European manufacturers could not hope to match.

The quality of competing motorcycles from Japan was especially important in comparison to the quality of Ducatis, which often suffered electrical problems and were plagued by poor paint and fiberglass. Recalls Jim Woods, who ran the Woods Motor Shop in Glendale, California, from 1976 to 1986, "The average guy didn't want to put up with the headaches. The manufacturing was very crude, compared to what was coming from the Japanese and the Germans."

So the inevitable happened.

Berliner says, "When we saw what was happening, we told Ducati we were going to fold. It was a wonderful, beautiful relationship. I wish it could have continued. But that would not have been right. You can lose money for one year, okay; but when you lose money for two years, you've got to stop. We were a private company, and everything else was factory subsidized. So in 1983, we closed."

And when dealers ran out of whatever stock they had on hand, that was the end of Ducati in America, at least for a while.

AH, BEAUTY. The Darmah SS used a German-built electronic ignition and a pair of huge, 40-mm Dell'Orto carbs to produce more than adequate horsepower and a wonderfully flat torque curve. At a time when Japanese bikes had horsepower without handling, this bike, to a few riders who understood its appeal, offered both those things.

FOUR

THE 1980S AND 1990S—
DUCATI REVITALIZED

The loss of the Berliner Motor Corp.'s distributor network was a defining moment for Ducati. The company was almost broke at home and completely without distribution in America. Further, for the first time since Ducati became a force in European motorcycling, it was without the services of Fabio Taglioni, who retired at the beginning of 1983 to devote himself to his beloved cacti.

A desultory effort was made in January 1983 to keep the motorcycles flowing through a Houston company called VM of America, formed to cooperate with Italy's IRI to coordinate imports from Italy. But that same year Mario Brighigna, who was running the company for Finmeccanica, announced that most of Ducati Meccanica would be liquidated, with its factories, equipment, and lands sold. But, he said, engine-building operations would remain active to provide powerplants for a new company called Cagiva. In a comic opera bit of schizophrenia, the resulting motorcycles would carry the Cagiva badge, but the engines would carry Ducati identification. When word of this reached American enthusiasts, it marked the first time most had heard of Cagiva.

HOTROD HEAVEN. The vaunted Ducati F1 came in several flavors. This one, from the Guy Webster collection, is a Montjuich. All used 750-cc Pantah engines in advanced states of tune. The F1 was based on the TT1 racebike. The earliest models, designated F1a, came with aluminum tanks, while the F1bs had steel tanks and slightly different paint schemes.

LIMITED EDITION. An ongoing Ducati tradition is to serialize its limited-production sportbikes. This one, the Webster Montjuich, is number 153. Today, the high-performance model of the 916 is available in SP5 designation, with that number increasing by one point for each model year of production. These, too, are serialized.

NOT WHAT THEY WANTED. Proof that the Italian view of style is different from the American view of style. The custom prototype sent to Italy came back looking like this, with the name "Indiana" arrayed on its flanks. To say that it was not a resounding sales success would be to indulge in understatement. Cycle World

It was good news for Ducati, which by now was building very little, except for the last few Hailwood Replicas, and a few 900 and 1000S2s. Joe Parkhurst, long departed from *Cycle World* but still deeply involved in the motorcycle industry, remembers what amounts to a final bit of tragicomedy: "They were concentrating on building four-cylinder diesel taxi engines for Fiat on the motorcycle production lines. When there were no bikes available for the U.S. market, that was why; they were busy building taxi motors. Here in the United States there was a big legal battle over who owned enormous stores of parts that had accumulated at several dealerships. The factory wanted them, the dealers didn't like the deal, and as I remember, these parts were in containers that were shipped all over

A DEVELOPMENT. As F1 production crippled along and Ducati decided to upgrade the early F1a model with the later F1b, the factory downgraded from expensive and easily damaged aluminum fuel tanks to cheaper-but-sturdier steel tanks. Other detail changes, including alternate paint schemes and several limited series of high-performance sub-lines— the Santa Monica and Montjuich, for instance— resulted. *Jeff Hackett*

the United States for quite a while as ownership was being contested."

Those parts came to rest first in Houston, and finally on the Los Angeles area premises of Cagiva North America, a company formed in 1982 by brothers Claudio and Gianfranco Castiglioni to distribute Cagiva motorcycle products in the United States. Cagiva North America was part of The Cagiva Group, an outgrowth of a company created in 1960 by the brothers' father, Giovanni Castiglioni, to manufacture luggage locks and hinges and other precision hardware.

By 1978 the brothers, both of them motorcycle enthusiasts, ran the company. That year they bought

the defunct Aermacchi/Harley-Davidson factory. Aermacchi originally built airplanes, and then motorcycles, in Varese, Italy, on the shore of Lago de Varese, a small lake between Lagos de Como and Maggiori in the Italian Lake District. (An entirely believable piece of lore has it that during Aermacchi's aircraft-building days, unsuccessful prototypes were pushed from the factory grounds into the lake, which is immediately adjacent.)

Taking syllables from their father's name and from Varese (Ca, Gi, and Va) the brothers named

REPRISE. When times are hard you use what you have, and that's just what Ducati did. It had the tooling to produce F1 frames and 750-cc Pantah engines. So it did. The result was the 1990 750 Sport, a stopgap machine meant to hold the fort until 851 production was in full song. The 750 Sport was an immensely likable motorcycle in spite of its much maligned Weber automotive carburetor and its 16-inch wheels. *Zack Miller Collection*

OVER THE TOP. A primary marker of the prevailing situation with Ducati ownership is that riders rarely leave their machines stock. This bike, owned by Californian Ed Marin and built by Pro Italia Motors in Glendale, California, is an 888 streetbike that has been lavished with Superbike race parts. Ducatis are supposed to be red? Right, unless they're Fly Yellow, an official Ferrari, and Ducati, color.

BREAK THE BANK. Marin's 888 is a rolling example of the way race parts can improve a streetbike. It rolled out of the factory with a Showa fork and lightweight alloy rims. It now wears an Ohlins racing fork and Marvic carbon-fiber racing wheels, a combination that greatly improves the way the bike steers and handles pavement imperfections.

the company Cagiva and immersed themselves in the motorcycle business, opportunistically buying up the rights to famous names such as Moto Morini and Ducati so they could position themselves to realize a long-held dream—build and sell a Cagiva-badged motorcycle.

Part of the Cagiva plan was finalized in June 1983 as the growth of Cagiva overlapped the fading of Ducati. Though it continued to assemble a few bikes from parts on hand, by 1984 the original, pre-Castiglioni Ducati was almost completely out of business, and the Castiglionis bought its remnants from the Italian government for a reported $5 million. Their plan was to sell two Ducati Pantah-powered motorcycles in the United States through Cagiva North America. These were the Cagiva Alazzurra, based on the Ducati Pantah SL and TL frames and engines, and the Cagiva Elefant, a Paris–Dakar–style explorer bike named for Cagiva's corporate symbol, a cartoon elephant. Both of these bikes were introduced to the public at the 1983 Milan Motorcycle Exposition.

Formation of the Ducati deal between Finmeccanica/IRI and Cagiva meant that Cagiva North America would distribute Ducati-powered motorcycles in the United States. That meant that after just a six-month period, VM of America was out of the motorcycle business.

It came near to meaning that Mike Berliner was back in the motorcycle business, as the Castiglioni Brothers figured that what had worked for Berliner before the collapse of Ducati would work again. But there was a problem.

Berliner recalls, "I didn't get along with younger brother (Claudio), whom I considered a playboy, a fast-speaking individual. The older brother, Gianfranco, was a decent, fine man, a quiet man. The younger brother is good looking, but the older knew what it was all about. They offered me the East Coast, and said they would put someone else on West Coast. I wouldn't do it unless I could be fully responsible for the entire United States."

UGLY DUCKLING. What we have here is failure to communicate the designer's intent to the buying public. It's a 750 Paso Limited, which came only in pearl white. Available in limited numbers, appreciated by a limited number of enthusiasts.

WISHFUL THINKING. One of the great strengths of the Italian motorcycle is also one of its great weaknesses: Designers sometimes are hired and given free rein to build their favorite projects. Massimo Tamburini's favored project was the Paso. The result was a bike that wasn't a sportbike and wasn't a touring bike. The bike was poorly received by enthusiasts until it was upgraded into the 907IE. Too late. The damage had been done. *Zack Miller Collection*

906 · PASO

Form and function. There's no doubt that the Paso is the style leader of the Ducati line. The latest generation sports a new 906cc engine—a liquid-cooled V-twin Desmo powerplant that raises existing standards of smoothness to new heights. Coupled with our silken-smooth six-speed transmission, this machine offers matchless performance.

We've modified Massimo Tamburini's exclusive body design with elements from our Grand Prix bike—specifically, new ducting to aid air flow to the radiators. And we slimmed down the Paso's profile for added aerodynamic efficiency.

Premium radial tires, fully adjustable suspension and all top-quality fasteners and components are part of the package that discriminating enthusiasts have come to expect from Ducati. Wherever it goes, the Paso attracts attention. Ride it, and redefine the motorcycling experience.

■ With our easy-to-read instrumentation, information never looked so good.

■ Impeccably perfect styling comes direct from our Grand Prix bikes.

Not allowing Berliner to resume his national distribution deal may have been an important mistake. As Schilling puts it, "Anytime you have that kind of interruption and disorganization, it really hurts. This act of interruption probably set Ducati back a number of years. Because whatever you thought of Berliner, he was here, present."

The people who took over responsibility at Cagiva North America weren't present, at least not at first; they were Italians transferred to the United States from Italy specifically to do the job. The first of them was Atillio Sandroni, hired in 1983 as director of operations for the company, which set itself up in Los Angeles.

Sandroni lasted less than a year and eventually returned to Italy to be replaced by Alberto and Daniella Carnelli, the husband a banker and the wife a marketing expert for the Italian fashion merchandiser Benetton. One of Sandroni's first acts had been to hire Joe Parkhurst's firm, Parkhurst Communications, to handle public relations and help with the introduction of the Alazzurra and Elefant. Parkhurst's deal with CNA was continued by the Carnellis.

The business developed slowly, Parkhurst says, partly because of confusion caused by the replacement of Sandroni by the Carnellis, and partly because the Carnellis moved very deliberately. Parkhurst recalls, "They were sharp, but slow, and they questioned a lot of things; they moved very hesitantly. But I thought they did a good job, and by the time they went back to Italy we had a lot of dealers."

Bruce Armstrong was hired to help keep those dealers happy and supplied with product. As dealer development manager from 1985 to 1988, when he left the company, he didn't have an easy job.

He now says of Ducati, "They dropped the ball in America. They knew they were going to phase out the bevel-drive V-twins, but they didn't have [a large-displacement engine] ready to replace it with. Also, the Castiglionis wanted to drop the Ducati name entirely. They wanted the Cagiva name on

CONTINUED ON PAGE 69

BEST IN CLASS. ADVICE: If you find a clean 907IE for sale, buy it. Embodying as it does the Paso concept come of age, the bike is balanced, comfortable, beautiful, and fast. Plus, it carries a passenger with aplomb, providing your passenger possesses aplomb.

RARE BEAST. Eager to begin beating the promotional drums for the 851, Ducati sent 10 of the beasts, in single-seat, European-spec form, to the United States in 1989. Dealers, who saw magazines tests of Ducatis they'd never received, were nonplused. *Cycle* magazine tested one of the bikes and gave it rave reviews in its September 1989 edition. *Zack Miller Collection*

851 · SPORT

No holds barred. The 851 never receives a casual glance—but it's not a casual motorcycle. *Cycle* magazine said, " …this is the most performance-intensive, street-going Ducati there has ever been."

A World Superbike Championship powerplant gives this machine its muscle.

We took the technology from our World Superbike Championship winner and turned it loose on the street. At its heart beats a Massimo Bordi-designed engine. Liquid cooling, a dry racing clutch, computer-controlled electronic fuel injection and four valve-per-cylinder Desmo heads make this Ducati the fastest production V-twin motorcycle ever to hit the street.

The 851 chassis is just as gutsy—with 42mm Marzocchi M1R adjustable racing forks in front and a fully adjustable Marzocchi single shock behind. The handling is so good *Cycle* called it "almost mystical."

Only a select few will ever own this limited-production, handmade machine. The ultimate sport bike, it's guaranteed to be the center of attention anywhere it goes.

Tested on a track, refined in a wind tunnel to achieve the ultimate in aerodynamics.

STREET SUPERBIKE! Finally, in 1991, the first of the 1990 851 Stradas began trickling into the United States. A glut of F1s ensued as diehard Ducati enthusiasts put those bikes up for sale to finance the purchase of 851s. This 851 Strada, owned by the author, was the first such bike to arrive in the United States, sent here by the factory for the purposes of a story in *Cycle World. Jon F. Thompson*

WIDEN THE LINE. With the 851 finally in production, Ducati still had the capacity to build standard air-cooled, two-valve engines. The result was continued production of the 750 Sport and the all-new 900 Super Sport, introduced to American audiences late in 1991. The 900SS was very warmly received and was still being sold in the United States in 1998 when European customers were slated to receive a significantly upgraded version known as the 944. *Zack Miller Collection*

LEFT: **STREET SUPERBIKE?** Fast for the street? All it took was money and connections. If you had both, you could own one of these, an 851 tricolor, a thinly disguised racebike offered in very limited numbers in the United States in 1988.

DUCATI

851 SPORT

907 PASO i.e.

IMPROVING WITH AGE. The line was little-changed for the 1991 model year, which this brochure photo touts. The 851 got a steel tank in place of the early aluminum unit, and it got upside-down Showa forks. And finally, the Paso concept was brought to maturity with the air-and-oil-cooled, fuel-injected 907IE, for which, ironically, the Paso name was dropped. *Zack Miller Collection*

CONTINUED FROM PAGE 64

everything. They kept sending us Alazzurras, bikes that looked like luggage."

So Armstrong and his dealers faced several problems.

The first was that the Alazzurra was a hard sell. It wasn't a Ducati, it was a Cagiva, and nobody knew what a Cagiva was. Though these Cagivas were powered by engines clearly marked with the Ducati name, that wasn't enough for American enthusiasts. And even though the bikes were well received by the American media—in September 1987 *Cycle World* Magazine published a memorable three-way comparison in which an Alazzurra, compared to a Kawasaki EX500 and a Moto Guzzi V65, received very high marks—this press reception wasn't enough to swing things Cagiva's way.

The second problem was that the bikes handled and stopped well, but had relatively low horsepower levels. Ducatis had always traded horsepower for handling, but now enthusiasts had access to a range of spectacular Japanese equipment that did everything well. All of them accelerated like there was no tomorrow. So now the Alazzurra's relative lack of power was a far bigger and more important problem than it might have been in the past.

Third, in a theme that continues to resound, dealers who could sell Alazzurras couldn't get enough bikes.

George Huebner worked under the Carnellis as director of operations from July 1985 through most of 1988. He recalls, "We just couldn't thrive, we didn't have any product. 'Always late but worth the wait,' that's the Italian national motto. 'It was shipped yesterday'—that meant they hadn't built it yet. They'd tell us, 'It's on the water.' And we'd wonder, 'Well, which water would that be? Like, the Bering Sea? Is it headed this way?'"

But lack of product, and the difficulties of communicating with the Italians, weren't the entire problems, Huebner continues: "We'd order specific mod-els and they'd ship us whatever they wanted. We took what we got. If we wanted it, fine; if not, we got it anyway.

"And the bikes they'd send us would have the wrong Vehicle Identification Numbers (VINs) stamped on them, and we'd have to go down to the Department of Motor Vehicles and dance around for a while to try to get that handled. At one point we had a whole warehouse full of Alazzurras that had to be titled as used motorcycles because the factory didn't read our faxes [explaining the United States' specific rules about the number of digits in VINs].

"We'd complain to the factory and they'd say, 'It's not a problem, you call someone.' And we'd ask ourselves, 'Like who, President Reagan?' The Italians didn't understand. It's not like you could go give some consigliere 6 billion lira and consider the problem solved. They didn't understand that doing business here in 50 separate states was like doing business in 50 Italies. I always thought that the powers in Italy believed they had some kind of papal dispensation from reality."

Huebner adds, "The Italians thrive on confusion, they live for it. They're wonderful people, but they just can't be satisfied with tranquillity."

Craig Morningstar, formerly an executive with Alfa Romeo in the United States, offers some insightful perspectives on the challenges of doing business with Italians. He says the difficulties involve basic differences in the way the two societies relate to problems.

"The Italians are pretty organized," Morningstar contends, "and they have their hierarchy. But Italians

NEXT: **RARE BIRD.** A generous dose of carbon fiber and stunning yellow livery made the 900 Superlight a favorite with the faithful. The short production run and limited availablility increases the 900SS variant's crowd-pleasing power. *Rich Chenet*

DUCATI DESMO

▼
Desmo domination. Powerful reasons to ride a Ducati.

There's no sound like a Desmo V-twin. Nothing so soothing as its primal, throaty growl. It's a light-weight, high revving engine that screams out on top like a Formula 1 racer. And powered Ducati to the 1990 World Superbike Championship.

The unique, Desmodromic valve train operates without the weight and resistance of valve springs. This unique mechanism ensures perfect valve actuation through the entire rev range, ingeniously eliminating dangerous valve float and bounce.

The result? Two-valve twins with higher valve acceleration rates than the four cylinder competitors they run with. And one four-valve Desmo engine that runs away from them all. Our no holds-barred, World Champion 851 Sport.

Ducati's performance engineering has always held a special mystique. Earned with Pro Twin and World Superbike titles on the most demanding race circuits. But best appreciated in the hands of the world's most envied sports riders: Ducati enthusiasts.

All Desmo four-strokes deliver their famous low end grunt and exceptionally smooth torque at every rpm level. All without exceeding stringent noise and emissions restrictions.

Our 851 Sport and 907 Paso i.e. take performance to an even higher level. Liquid cooling and newly advanced computer fuel injection give them endless power and instant response. The World Champion 851 Sport powers up to 10,000 rpm—scorching the quarter mile in just over 11 seconds.

The 6-speed 900 Super Sport and 5-speed 750 Sport are marvels of mechanical simplicity. Their carbureted two-valve, 90° V-twins feature dependable digital CDI ignition. Hydraulically controlled dry racing clutches assure positive engagement right up to redline.

Ducati surrounds every Desmo engine with a sculpted aerodynamic shape so beautiful, even the wind can't resist. Hand-rubbed, ruby red paint. And style that's become the benchmark for sports motorcycles. Once you've experienced the thrill and inner calm of a Desmo-powered Ducati, you'll agree with *Motorcyclist Magazine's* editors—"These are motorcycles that inflame the cerebral pleasure centers, before they tickle your intellect."

**1990 World Superbike Champion
1990 AMA GP1 Champion
1990 AMA GP2 Champion**

TROPHY TIME. When engineer Massimo Bordi was given the task of advancing Ducati's sales and racing fortunes, this was the result: a liquid-cooled, fuel-injected, four-cam, 90-degree V-twin that included a six-speed transmission. Though the Ducati eight-valve, as it's known, saw its first racing laps in 751-cc form, racing versions of the engine now displace 996 cc and produce more than 140 rear-wheel horsepower. *Zack Miller Collection*

basically are anarchists. An Italian told me once, 'In each man there is a republic.' Also, they're very adaptable, much more so than Americans, and they love to work from crisis control. For instance, we've got a real thing about punctuality. And if you're trying to sell something, and it hasn't arrived for you to sell, that's a problem. But the Italian point of view is that if dinner's late, does whining help? No, not really."

Thus, Morningstar contends, the American way of doing business put Americans in direct conflict with the Italian way of doing business.

Schilling, of *Cycle* Magazine, remembers a situation that further illustrates the challenges Americans faced when dealing with the Italian method of problem-solving. He says, "When we were doing the racing program, we were trying to get some special parts. We ordered them, they didn't arrive. We inquired where they were, and the famous telex arrives. It says, 'In these days we send. . . .' Now, what does this mean? It means they will probably send the parts at their earliest convenience, and hopefully that will correspond with our convenience. Those five words, 'In these days we send. . . .' sort of catch it all. It's very perplexing. They've got a different point of view about how life is lived. They don't take commerce too seriously. It comes, and it goes."

generation Ducatis built on a classic ciple: performance is the final measure.

Dominating most every pack of riders, is one way out front aboard our 851 Sport. uid-cooled, four-valve Desmo twin has six ds. All of them fast forward. 17" Brembo els, Ducati upside down forks and adjustable s rear suspension straighten out the twisti- ads. It's the most aggressive, rewarding racer you've ever laid eyes on—dubbed by rcyclist Magazine, "the most beautiful two- eled creation on this or any other planet." ecause it's a Ducati, its real beauty is rmance.

The 907 Paso i.e. may just be the most exciting big bore left on earth. From its domi- nant, GP-inspired bodywork and perimeter frame to its light, confident steering, it is a sport touring bike unequaled in style, comfort and handling. *Cycle World* called it, "a rider's delight, likely to become a classic in its own time."

The power of its 904cc, 6-speed Desmo V-twin is handled with amazing grace by Michelin radials, adjustable anti-dive Marzocchi forks and rising rate rear suspension. And if you think the 907 Paso i.e. is a visual stopper, test the brakes. Dual 300mm floating front discs and a massive rear caliper haul you down from speed fast and fade-free.

You take sports riding seriously. Ducati takes it to the street.

Ducati is the dominant force in serious sports machines that make getting there all the fun. The sheer burst of our 900 Super Sport will have you grinning ear-to-ear. Its oil-cooled, 6-speed V-twin is cradled in a lightweight chromoly frame. Just one of the many advances to traditional Ducati design. Up front, new Ducati upside down forks hug the road respon- sively. Our engineers also pulled out all the stops to design new, lighter stainless steel disc brakes with even more progressive action. In back, an adjustable Ohlins shock delivers true rising rate suspension. It's pure power and handling,

wrapped in a body that turns impressive figures in the wind tunnel, and heads on the street.

At just 396 pounds dry, our 750 Sport with its two-valve, oil-cooled V-twin Desmo engine runs with bikes with twice as many cylinders. Marzocchi forks and adjustable rear shock let you tune Ducati's F1 suspension for your favorite set of switchbacks. Our 750 Sport is the eminently affordable Ducati that introduces world class performance to a whole new gener- ation of riders.

In an era of look-alike bikes stamped out by assembly lines, Ducatis are a rare tribute to what patience, human hands and commitment can build: high performance sports machines of uncompromising quality.

MOVING PRODUCT. Ducati sought to tie the tame little 750 Sport to the performance and charisma of the 851 with ads like this. It didn't work. Note that though the factory calls the 851 an eight-valve, Ducati's American arm referred to it as a four-valve motorcycle. Both descriptions are, in their own way, correct. *Zack Miller Collection*

The problem, of course, is that once commerce goes, it's very difficult indeed to get it to come again. And with the Alazzurra, commerce very nearly fled for good. The company was saved by the nick-of-time 1985 introduction of a machine that could be seen as a fire-breathing, hard-edged Ducati, even if it did carry the Cagiva logo. It was the F1, an all-new

chassis using the now-trademark trellis-type frame and carrying a 750-cc version of the Pantah desmo engine. And in its green, red, and white livery, it was beautiful. The bike began as a racebike, a model known as the TT1. It was converted into a streetbike by the addition of milder cams, lights, and a battery- operated ignition system.

RARE NO MORE. For most of Ducati's history, actually seeing the bikes parked at the races was unusual. These days, thanks to an overwhelming acceptance of the eight-valve bikes, finding them parking amidst a crush of Hondas and Harleys isn't hard at all.

Even then, Huebner says, "We had a hard time with them. First, the F1s were only quasi-legal; the factory sent them all in with weird numbers, and we had to renumber them and get waivers and exclusions because they weren't supposed to be streetbikes. Also, they were a hard sell to Ducatiphiles because the F1s had that Cagiva elephant on them. And to those guys, buying one was like having your sister marry some kind of weird guy."

As in the past, the motorcycling press fell in love with this latest offering. After all, what was not to like? As with the first 851s, when they appeared in 1991, the early F1s even appeared with aluminum tanks, a badge of their competition heritage and intent. Steve Anderson, a staffer at *Cycle World* Magazine at the

time, entered the magazine's road-test F1 in the 1986 running of La Carrera, the street race from Ensenada to San Filipe, in Baja, California, changing the bike's oil and tires, and giving it nothing more than a quick tuneup. He won the event overall.

In the same issue that carried the story of Anderson's Mexico triumph, *Cycle World* ran its roadtest of the bike Anderson rode to victory. What the test said was that things finally had changed with Ducati. First, it said that Ducati's F1 was to the rest of the sportbike crowd as a Rolling Stones concert is to Muzak. And second, it noted that in performance testing, the magazine's F1 had blitzed through the quarter-mile in 11.87 seconds, and that it had a top

MORE IS LESS. Ayrton Senna was a champion, maybe the finest driver Formula One roadracing had ever seen. He was also a Ducati enthusiast. Prior to his death during the 1994 running of the San Marino Grand Prix at Imola, Italy, he'd agreed to help design a special-edition 916. He'd signed the paperwork and agreed on the color scheme. By the next weekend after that signing, he was dead at Tamburelo Corner. The 916 Senna went into limited production with special colors and special brakes but without the high-spec tuning that was projected.

speed of 136 miles per hour. This, in 1986, was impressive performance from any motorcycle, let alone a V-twin whose engine displaced just 750 cc.

Finally, it was proof from the most trusted of sources that Ducatis no longer were slow—even if their chassis carried the puzzling Cagiva nameplate.

As a result, Ducati diehards began adopting these raucous machines, and began building into them attributes each owner felt his bike lacked. For there was a ready lineup of aftermarket suppliers with even louder exhausts, bigger jets for the Dell'Orto carbs, hotter cams, and bigger pistons with higher compression.

All this, however, impressive as it was, constituted but a minor breakthrough, and finally this difficulty of selling Cagivas became impressed on the Castiglionis. They decided that the next motorcycle would be a Ducati.

That next motorcycle was a landmark for an additional reason: It was designed by Massimo Tamburini, whom the Castiglionis lured away from Bimota, the Italian specialty manufacturer he helped found. Tamburini's first brief was to design a new Ducati using the existing Pantah 750 engine. This he did, naming it the Paso after Renzo Pasolini, an Italian roadrace star killed at Monza in 1973.

QUICKER IS QUICK ENOUGH. For some riders, the 916 is fine just the way it is. This bike, owned by Californian Gary Becker, got the yellow numberplates of the racing 916s and benefits from an upgraded chip in its engine-management computer, which controls its ignition and fuel injection. It also wears Marchesini wheels.

The bike was said to be Tamburini's dream bike, an idea he'd toyed with since he was a design student, and it pointed to the passion and sense of personal mission Ducati's designers so often seem to have. The Paso, introduced to the enthusiast public in late 1985 at the Milan Motorcycle Exposition, was a departure for several reasons. First, it presaged a changed company philosophy that would see a wide variety of high-performance models all available at the same time. Second, though it used the same basic 750-cc powerplant as the F1, the Paso was a kinder, gentler Ducati, with all-enclosing bodywork and comfortable seating for both rider and passen-

ger. And third, though it carried Cagiva's elephant logo, the name on the bike was Ducati.

The Castiglionis understood the position their company found itself in, and they pulled out all the stops to give this new bike, their first pure Ducati, the best possible reception. They did this by allowing a contingent of the motorcycling press to visit Italy where they could poke, prod, and ride the bike, and also poke, prod, and question the bike's designer.

Cycle World magazine reported, in the headline to its story, that sportbikes were alive and well in Varese, the northern Italian city in which Cagiva retained its headquarters. The Paso wasn't exactly

READY AND RED. The World Superbike championship, run for the first time in 1988, was won its first two years by Fred Merkel aboard a Honda RC30. Ducati, working hard on the 851, watched and waited, and in 1990 entered Frenchman Raymond Roche on an 851 Corsa. Roche, seen here leading Giancarlo Falappa, won the 1990 championship, established Ducati's competitive expectations, and set the tone for advertising brochures like this one. *Zack Miller Collection*

LATE, GREAT. Through much of the 1980s, if you were a Ducatisti and a racing enthusiast—and certainly, if you were one, you were the other—you followed the exploits of Jimmy Adamo. He's seen here cranking his Ducati through one of the corners in Daytona's infield in 1987. He died there in a crash during the running of the 1993 Daytona 200 Superbike race. Thanks to Arai, his helmet design lives on. *Tom Riles*

UNLOVED. His wife probably loves him, and also his mother. But American race fans didn't much care for racer Carl Fogarty, who came to Daytona in 1995 after telling the motorcycling press that he didn't care for Americans, didn't like America, and was going to kick everybody's ass and go home. Scott Russell won at Daytona that year, but Foggy went on to win the World Superbike Championship. *Tom Riles*

WAAAY OVER. Fogarty won his '95 World Superbike championship by means of a superb motorcycle, and also superb riding skills. He demonstrates here just how far a modern roadrace motorcycle can lean, thanks to very sticky tires, terrific chassis technology, and balls as big as watermelons. *Tom Riles*

a sportbike, but that seemed not to matter. What did matter was that charismatic V-twin motorcycles were being produced under the Ducati name. *Cycle World* claimed the Paso was destined to be one of the motorcycling world's most exciting performers. As noted, however, the Paso lacked the verve of a pure sportbike. Riders demanding extreme sporting characteristics in their mounts still made up the small but determined core of Ducati's buyers. So the Paso never was completely adopted by the faithful.

In the meantime Cagiva undertook two other notable projects. In the first, Cagiva North America, on the lookout for a way to sell product, decided to take a crack at the custom/cruiser market. In 1986 Parkhurst, still deeply involved in Cagiva North America, arranged for an unsold Alazzurra to be delivered to AMA racer and bike-builder Dallas Baker, who ran a Kawasaki dealership in Southern California's Orange County.

NAKED. Fogarty's Fast by Ferracci racebike outside its Daytona garage with its clothes off reveals . . . not much. Until you look closely. Notice, for instance, the magnesium swingarm, lengthened a few millimeters to perfect the 916's chassis geometry, and thus its handling. Such swingarms are available to street riders willing to shell out the bucks. Some are. *Tom Riles*

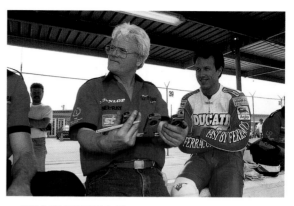

BRAIN TRUST. The most talented tuner of his day and the finest rider on the circuit? In the early years of the 1990s that might have been Eraldo Ferracci, left, and Doug Polen. Best bike on the circuit? No question: Polen's 888-cc 851, made fast by Ferracci. *Tom Riles*

Parkhurst recalls, "Dallas was a fine craftsman, and when he was done with the bike it looked great, with all the right styling cues, right down to the Harleyesque air cleaners. It was really cute."

The bike was shipped to Italy in the hope that it would be reproduced for sale here, with objections from Bruce Armstrong. He recalls, "I told Alberto Carnelli the bike should not be brought here. We needed red bikes with loud exhaust pipes."

The Indiana came anyway, and the result was disaster.

Parkhurst says of the bike Ducati delivered, "It was just awful, quite different from the prototype we sent them. We were all of us very upset; it seemed like we just couldn't tell the Italians anything. They figured they already knew it all."

The Italians certainly knew what they wanted to call this bike.

Parkhurst recalls, "They wanted to call it an Indian, but they couldn't. Well, they were obsessed by Indiana Jones, so they called it the Indiana. Boy, did that bike fall flat on its face."

The other notable project was the one that carried Ducati to its current high visibility and success. Back in Bologna, a young engineer named Massimo Bordi had donned the mantle of the retired Taglioni. He was at work on the engine that would power Ducati into whatever the future held for it. This was a new, eight-valve, liquid-cooled, fuel-injected engine—the prototype of the 851 engine which became, after extensive development, the 916 engine. In the course of his engineering education, Bordi had submitted a thesis on just such an engine. This theoretical engine used the Ford-Cosworth DFV V-8 as its model—not a bad model, as to that date the DFV, used in three-liter form in Formula One car racing and downsized for use in Indycar racing, was the most successful race motor ever conceived.

This new engine was built in considerable secrecy. Parkhurst remembers visiting the factory and being told by Taglioni, hanging out at the factory then as now as a kind of engineer emeritus, that Ducati never would build a four-valve head.

SUPERTUNER. When the 851/888 reached the end of its development cycle, Ducati's fortunes advanced with the advent of the 916. Ferracci's didn't. The man, seen here working on one of his 916 racebikes, continued with fine equipment but with riders who were not of the caliber of Polen or of Troy Corser, who rode and won for Ferracci before joining the World Superbike wars as a Ducati factory pilot. *Tom Riles*

Nevertheless, this revolutionary engine was being built, complete with desmodromic valve actuation and an engine-management system adapted from a system developed by Weber-Marelli for the Ferrari F40 supercar. The engine made its debut in 751-cc form at the 1986 running of the Bol 'd Or, an endurance race held each fall in France. It was seen again, displacing 851 cc, at the 1987 Battle of the Twins race in Daytona Beach in the hands of former world champion Marco Lucchinelli. It won the race and in doing so set the stage for Ducati in World Superbike.

World Superbike was designed by the International Motorcycling Federation (FIM), the sport's world-sanctioning body, for motorcycles powered by 750-cc four-cylinder engines. Yet the FIM recognized that horsepower largely depends on the amount of fuel-air mixture that flows through an engine. It recognized that fours, by the fact of having more pistons and valves, can process more mixture than twins. In an effort to establish parity between fours and twins, the FIM promulgated rules that gave twins a 25-percent displacement advantage over fours, and also a small weight advantage. Thus, a Ducati 851, 888, 916, 955, or 995, remains a 750-class Superbike as long as it is powered by just two cylinders.

CORSER FOR COURSES. Aussie Troy Corser came along in 1994 to follow in Polen's footsteps. Shown here at Pomona, California, aboard a Fast by Ferracci 888 during an AMA Superbike event, he was so successful that the Castiglionis offered him a factory World Superbike ride for 1995. He took it and gained a World Superbike championship.

RACEBIKE BASICS. A 916 Corsa stripped. Not much to it without its tank and bodywork, except a 140-horsepower engine, big-time brakes and suspension, and Marchesini wheels. If it isn't chrome-moly, it's aluminum, titanium, or carbon fiber.

Bordi's great gift involved efficiency. His engines were able to process their air-fuel mixture more efficiently than the fours—that is, they were able to flow more mixture and make more horsepower. Indeed, the extreme competitiveness of Ducatis in World Superbike pushed the Japanese manufacturers and their race teams to find more horsepower. As they did, the Ducatis gradually approached the ultimate limit, set by the FIM's rules, of 1,000 cc.

All this, however, remained in the future, a future that nobody at Cagiva North America had any hint of. The 851, which eventually was introduced to the public in Milan in the fall of 1987, didn't make it to the United States in street-legal form until June 1990, when a single 851 Strada [which now makes its home in the author's garage] was sent to *Cycle World* magazine for a road test. The previous year, ten 851SPs [one of which was road-tested by *Cycle*] had been sent, but these were single-seaters with European VINs, meant strictly for racetrack use. These were of little benefit to the struggling dealers, so for now, at least, all the dealers and their customers knew was that the Paso was the Next Great Ducati.

The flow of Pasos didn't begin until late 1986, a year after the bike was introduced at the Milan Motorcycle Exposition. And then just three bikes showed up. A real, predictable flow didn't begin until much later. Indeed, *Cycle World* magazine didn't run its first road test of the Paso until its October 1987 issue. Given the magazine's two-to-three-month lead time, that suggests it didn't get a test bike until the summer of 1987.

George Huebner recalls, "We kept thinking that when the Paso finally became available that it would be the ticket, the neatest thing anybody had seen. But it turned out it wasn't a Ducati freak's kind of bike. It wasn't hard-edged enough."

By the time Pasos finally started to flow to Cagiva North America, the company had another problem. In 1987 the Castiglionis acquired Husqvarna, the respected Swedish dirtbike manufacturer. That acqui-

sition meant moving Husqvarna's American operations from its building in San Diego to the Cagiva North American facility in Gardena, near Los Angeles.

During the course of the move, a part of the Husqvarna hardware that made the trip was a computer that contained Husqvarna's records. Huebner says, "We were trying to put Cagiva on that computer. It was not altogether an amiable takeover of Husky, and some disgruntled employee down there planted a [virus] in the computer. On a certain date everything just cratered, and the entire computer turned to gibberish. A lot of records never were recovered. For instance, there weren't very many F1s brought into the United States, maybe 50 or 60 F1As and maybe 100 F1Bs, but now we couldn't tell, because the records were destroyed."

Additionally, because of the loss of its record-keeping system, Cagiva North America lost track of a number of its motorcycles that were off-premises at the time this disaster occurred. Some stayed off-premises forever, because nobody at CNA knew the locations of all the bikes that needed to be called in.

At least the company was receiving some recognition in the enthusiast press. Huebner recalls, "By the time I left, there was a bit more credibility just because there was some product. We were getting ink. We were getting some word out there, but still we couldn't back it up with product. If we did have product it was at a ridiculous price. We had a few F1s, and if you lived in Tennessee or somewhere like that you could maybe get them registered and put on the street. We had Pasos, but they had that Weber automotive carburetor, and the carb was all screwed up. Plus, we had a couple of flagship 851s, and that was it."

Help remained on the horizon. Ducati decided to trade off the name of the much-loved 750 Sport of the 1970s. To do this, it slotted into the chrome-moly spaceframe of the F1 the 750-cc, Weber-carbureted engine of the Paso and wrapped the result in smooth, red-and-silver (and in Europe, red-and-blue) fiberglass fairings. Word of this bike leaked to

HEAD SHOP. Things at the factory sometimes are done in small batches, like these four-valve heads, for instance, all lined up and waiting for final assembly.

the press in 1988, and it was introduced to the U.S. market, in extremely limited numbers, in 1990.

Shortly after the 750 Sport was introduced in Europe, word of an enlarged Paso leaked out. This was the 906 Paso, introduced as a 1989 model at the IFMA Motorcycle Exhibition in Cologne in late 1988, and made available in the United States for the 1990 model year. This bike was lackluster in many ways, but it marked the creativity with which Bordi was rummaging through Ducati's parts bins back in Bologna. It used the cases of the 851, and air-cooled cylinders and two-valve-heads modeled after those of the 750. The bike's engine, which displaced 904 cc—Bordi told anyone who asked that he named the bike the 906 because it was a 900-class machine with a 6-speed transmission—was a wonderfully torquey device, and it excelled at pulling around a sport-touring rider and passenger, which was precisely its design mission. Its major drawback concerned stiff Marzocchi suspension and 16-inch wheels and tires. At one time the rage in Grand Prix racing, these were not suited for the street, and many riders changed the wheels on their Pasos and 750 Sports, which also had 16-inch wheels, to aftermarket 17s. Nevertheless, with this additional new model, things were looking up.

And then came another upheaval.

In early 1988 Cagiva North America pulled up its Los Angeles roots and moved, lock, stock, and desmodromics, to Fairfield, New Jersey. Parkhurst recalls, "Ernesto Vettore (who had operated Alfa-

PRESS DAY AT IFMA. How do we know? It's possible to see open floor, and there's space between the displays. When the show—billed as the largest motorcycle show in the world—opens to the public, you will not be able to see the bikes for the crush of humanity.

Romeo's operation in America) was sent over to run the place. He'd convinced the Castiglionis he could sell a lot more bikes. Well, that just wasn't possible. We couldn't get any more. In any case the Carnellis were sent back to Italy in disgrace, accused of embezzling money, and I lost my deal with Cagiva, accused of paying the Carnellis a kickback out of my contract fee. Of course I didn't, and those two, the Carnellis, were completely honest."

George Huebner agrees with Parkhurst's assessment. He says, "Alberto and Daniella were the salt of the earth. They were just wonderful people. It just seemed that after they left the new management had it in for them. A lot of files and data were destroyed to make them look bad." And Huebner says that the Carnelli's departure from Cagiva North America meant his departure as well. "I was the chief American under the Carnellis, so I had a giant target painted on my back. Finally I just left." So did Parkhurst, along with dealer development manager Armstrong.

Dealer Jim Woods offers a different perspective on the 1988 upheaval. He remembers, "The Carnellis were nice people, but they were not business people. When Mr. Vettore took over, he hired some expertise. He was good for CNA. He got better dealers into the network. He was a businessman. He didn't know motorcycles, but he knew business, and he appreciated good ideas that helped the system work better."

Whatever else can be said about Vettore's tenure at Cagiva North America, once he got there, things started happening—though whether that was due to good management, good staff, good luck, or the alignment of the planets remains a subject of more than a little disagreement.

What cannot be argued, however, is the importance to the company of its astounding racing successes, for those successes fueled the sales of the flagship eight-valve models. These were the 851, the 888—which used a slightly enlarged engine, improved suspension components and minimally revised styling—and the 916.

The 916, currently Ducati's sporting flagship, was an almost completely new motorcycle that reflected a significant rethink on the part of Massimo Tamburini, its designer. Tamburini made the bike much smaller than its predecessors, using a significantly revised 916-cc V-twin engine, and a new Weber-Marelli engine management system cradled in an all-new chrome-moly tubular frame. He aggressively centralized the bike's mass to give it a low polar moment of inertia, which made it even more nimble than its predecessors had been. To make the 916 racetrack-friendly, Tamburini made sure the engine, cooling system, and single-side swingarm [used despite threats from Honda, which unsuccessfully contended that it held exclusive patents on the design] could be removed as a unit, a step that makes trackside engine changes extremely quick and easy. Finally, he covered the result with the most avant garde bodywork anybody had ever seen on a motorcycle.

The result, of course, was instant success. Enthusiasts—even those who were not part of the hard-core family of Ducati owners—immediately embraced the 916. Available in its first several years in very limited numbers, it was nevertheless the machine that sportbike enthusiasts most wanted to own. And why not? It worked, as magazine testers and roadracers soon discovered, every bit as well as its very stylish bodywork and advanced technical specification promised it would.

Here's why: As with the F1, every member of the eight-valve family of bikes was designed as a racebike first—an indicator of the importance of Superbike racing to Ducati—and developed from its high-strung competitive form into a reliable and usable streetbike. Unlike the Japanese machines, which were designed as streetbikes and developed into racebikes, the Ducatis instantly shone on a racetrack. The considerable racing successes of this family of bikes; their exclusive, limited-production nature, and their gorgeous, drop-dead styling, made them the machines American enthusiasts coveted.

BRUSHED MONSTER. Randy King of southern California wanted an M900 Monster that wasn't like anybody else's. So he ordered up sheet-metal finish that includes brushed metal and a few bits of intelligent engine work performed by Jim Woods. *Jon F. Thompson*

A primary architect of Ducati's racing success in America, beginning with the 851 and continuing through the current 996 cc 916s, was Eraldo Ferracci, an engine-builder and former drag-racer who runs a small firm in Pennsylvania called Fast by Ferracci. Prior to Ferracci's involvement, racer Jimmy Adamo, ultimately killed while racing his Ducati Superbike at Daytona, was the Ducati standard-bearer in the United States, but Adamo had little factory support.

That lack of support changed when Ferracci got involved. He took a look at the first 851s and liked what he saw. Instead of going to Cagiva North America to talk about a racing deal, he went to Massimo Bordi. Bordi liked what he heard. The pair made their deal, and one result of that deal was that in 1988, Ferracci's Ducati 851, ridden by Dale Quarterley, won the American Motorcyclist Association's ProTwins championship.

The most important stipulation of his deal with Bordi, Ferracci says, was that he would refrain from making wholesale alterations to the bike. Instead, he would race the bike as it came to him so the factory engineers could accurately gauge the quality and direction of their work. Ferracci says, "We did that, and it worked real well."

FAST MONSTER. Ducati Monsters have at least as much custom and hot rod equipment available for them as Harley-Davidsons do. That suited country-music artist Lyle Lovett just fine. He ordered up this bike from Earl Campbell at Pro Italia Motors in Glendale, California, to emulate a project bike Campbell built for *Cycle World*.

Ferracci was, however, given the freedom to do detail tuning such as porting and flowing cylinder heads, but the rest of the engineering was done under factory control. His Fast by Ferracci racebikes were ridden first by Quarterley and later by Doug Polen, who captured the 1991 and 1992 World Superbike championships and the 1993 AMA Superbike title on FBF Ducatis. After that, a string of less well-known riders took them to somewhat less successful results, as the factory shifted its emphasis to World Superbike.

Said Ferracci, "I stuck with whatever Bordi said. I followed their line, and it was really great. We had a 100 percent understanding."

There was no such sweetness and light with Cagiva North America, however. In 1990 and 1991 Ferracci became involved in a CNA promotional program that involved building a series of 750 Sports to racing specification. He says of his relationship with Cagiva North America and Ernesto Vettore during this project, "Whatever you make, you gotta make it free. Whatever he gives you, you've got to pay. He just didn't believe in the racing program; his fear was that it jeopardized the business."

But it didn't hurt sales of 750 Sports. Though beautiful, light, and nimble, these bikes languished after the introduction of the 851 in spite of glowing press reviews. But with the promise of performance improvements from Ferracci's racetrack modifications—these included substituting individual motorcycle carburetors for the troublesome Weber two-barrel automotive unit, and adding high-lift cams and a high-performance exhaust system—interest in these tidy little bikes rose somewhat.

But interest in the 750s never grew to the point that it rivaled the race-wrought interest in the 851s. These booming, bright-red V-twins brought a new dimension to American racetracks, not least because like racing Ferraris, they retained their signature Italian racing-red paint. Additionally, their characteristic basso-profundo full-throttle roar—half exhaust note and half intake noise—intrigued and delighted enthusiasts and race fans. The fact that these bikes consistently beat the Kawasakis, Hondas, Yamahas, and Suzukis, however, was what cemented the deal.

Underscoring Ducati's traditional exclusivity were the prices for the eight-valve bikes. The first 851 Stradas retailed in 1990 for nearly $11,000, and every year after 1990 the price climbed a bit until the 916, released in 1994, retailed for nearly $16,000—more than twice what a competitive Japanese sportbike sold for. Well-heeled enthusiasts willing to spend the money applied deposits and waited for bikes to be delivered to dealerships.

Once delivered, very few of these bikes remained stock. Thanks to their on-board computers and to the ready availability of aftermarket parts, it was easy to develop a stock 90-horsepower 851, 93-horsepower 888, or 102-horsepower 916 into something that resembled a racebike. Just add an aftermarket high-performance computer chip and a free-flow exhaust, and you had the first step. For step two, add high-lift cams and high-compression pistons. To go whole hog and recreate a full-on Superbike for the street, just have Ferracci build you an engine and add the upgraded suspension and brake components. Or, short-circuit all this and buy an SP version with its few extra horsepower and upgraded chassis, or, even better, an 851/888/916 Corsa—the factory racebike

DETAIL INFORMATION. In stock form, Monsters have only a speedometer and warning lights. Lovett's bike uses this aftermarket instrument panel which includes a tachometer and a carbon-fiber mounting plate.

that came complete with a race kit, and put that on the street. These 140-horsepower bikes, without lights or starter, obviously are wildly illegal. But they represent precisely the course chosen by a few adventurous, performance-crazed enthusiasts.

This tremendous interest in the eight-valve Ducatis—with enthusiasts eager to get their hands on anything the factory built and willing to pay a premium price for it—should have translated to success, growth, and stability for Ducati. It did not.

The reason it didn't, Ferracci believes, is that, "They tried to grow too rapidly. To keep up with demand they built another assembly line, bought this and that, moved this around, so they never had any profit. Also, when you try to double the number of motorcycles you're building, your suppliers have to be able to go along with you. They've got to be able to hire more people and buy more material. And there was no capital for that. Everything's got to grow together instead of working with what you've got. Now, with this [investment from the Texas Pacific Group] they have more capital and maybe they can do a little better job."

MORE IS BETTER. In stock form, the engine in Lovett's Monster produced about 70 horsepower. When Campbell was done with it, it made 91 horsepower at its rear wheel, thanks to increased capacity, larger carburetors, high compression, and many other details.

One thing that can't be argued is that as the Castiglionis got their financial and manufacturing feet under them, the flow of product to the United States, and the variety of that product, began to expand. Sales rose from almost nil in the late 1980s to about 800 in 1990, to a peak in 1995 of about 3,500 units from a total production of about 20,000 motorcycles. That represents about 1.7 percent of the 203,000 motorcycles sold in the United States in 1995.

Yet there was considerable unrest among Ducati's dealers because of the prices they were paying for their motorcycles. Armstrong explains, "The Italians don't understand the concept of price protection. If you sell a dealer a product for $10, you have to guarantee him that if the product doesn't sell at that price, causing you to lower the price when selling the same product to other dealers, you guarantee the first dealer will be reimbursed the difference between what he paid for the product and what the others paid for it. The Japanese and Germans do this, but the Italians don't. I fought with them over this through my whole tenure at Cagiva North America."

Despite a certain amount of dealer unhappiness with CNA policies, and thanks in large measure to Ducati's success on roadracing tracks around the world, the Ducati model line grew and evolved in the late 1980s and early 1990s as never before. The fuel-injected 907ie was a new family member, tracing its ancestry through the 851 to the Pasos. In this bike,

MONSTER EXTREME. This M900 Monster is proof that some riders are never satisfied. Its standard four-valve engine was discarded in favor of a 926-cc eight-valve World Superbike engine capable of about 140 horsepower. Monster is the right name for it. *Jon F. Thompson*

finally, the Paso concept was fully developed and refined. Using a considerably upgraded chassis and brakes, and of course, the 851's fuel-injection system and the 17-inch wheels that now even the Grand Prix racers had adopted, this bike offered traditional Ducati performance with heretofore unseen riding comfort. In both those categories, it was fully competitive with Honda's vaunted VFR750, acknowledged as the best sport-touring bike then available. By now the Paso was largely discredited in the eyes of enthusiasts, so for the 907ie the name Paso was dropped. It followed the introduction of 851 in the United States, and in spite of the acclaim with which that bike was met, found a small but enthusiastic cadre of supporters.

So did the 851, and where the 907ies sold slowly, the 851s moved out of dealerships as quickly as they arrived—indeed, some dealers had long lists of buyers who had laid down deposit money long before the first 851s arrived here. With production so small that no more than a few hundred 851s ever made it to the United States in a single production year, Ducati sold every bike it could send, thanks to the bike's racetrack successes and its incredible bright-red presence. And after a few years this bike was upgraded with improved suspension and a slightly larger engine to become the 888, which was somewhat more refined than the original 851 but not much faster. The 888 was superseded for the 1995 model year by the 916,

A WHOLE LOTTA' HIGH TECH. The gold-colored casting you see is magnesium. Note that the radiator is curved, very much a racing piece. This engine powered a racebike ridden by Austrian Superbike champion Andy Meklau before it was shoe-horned into this Monster. *Jon F. Thompson*

and that machine was remarkably superior to anything that had come before it.

With the exceptions of the Paso and 907IE, all of these are legitimate offspring of the original 750 Super Sport. They're light, nimble sport machines developed originally as racebikes. As such, they put a premium on ultimate performance at considerable cost to rider comfort. Additionally, all were available as biposto (dual-seat) Strada, or monoposto (single-seat) SP supersport and full-on racing Corsa models—the first with a single fuel-injector per cylinder, and the latter two with dual injectors per cylinder as well as other high-performance features that include alternate computer chips and exhaust systems.

As a nod to a graying body of Ducati enthusiasts who wanted machines a little more comfortable and a little less intimidating than the hard-edged eight-valve models, the factory created several versions of a bike that was a little easier to live with. This was the 900 Super Sport. This machine was once again proof of

Bordi's creativity at making very fine and very different motorcycles by using parts already in production at the Bologna factory. Bordi again used the 851's engine cases atop which he mounted a set of air-cooled cylinders and two-valve heads, and a pair of Mikuni carburetors. He slotted the result into a frame very like that of the 1990 750 Sport—a development, remember, of the F1's frame; he clad this in sexy red bodywork; added a relaxed, semi-upright riding position; and stood back.

From the beginning, the 900SS was a hit. It featured comfortable ergonomics, and performance that placed a premium on mid-range over peak-rpm power. These machines, all air-cooled and all using two-valve heads, were freed from the hated Weber carburetor featured on the 750 and 900 Pasos and 750 Sport—this thanks to changes in Italy that finally allowed foreign content in Italian product. If there was a single complaint about these bikes, it was that they were overgeared for use on American roads, with sixth gear not being really usable until the speedometer touched 75 to 80 miles per hour. Owners soon learned that the cure for this was a gearing change made possible by installing a slightly larger-than-stock rear sprocket.

In addition to the base 900SS SP, which currently offers a variety of lightweight pieces, the 900 line eventually included the 900SS CR, a price-leader version with a steel swingarm instead of the standard aluminum piece. Another variation, the exclusive and short-lived 900SS Superlight, was swathed in yellow livery and sported an array of lightweight carbon-fiber accessories. Ducati also offered a restyled 750 Sport based on 900SS bodywork but with a quarter-fairing instead of the full-coverage piece.

The 900 progeny also included the E900 Elefant explorer bike, essentially a 900SS with off-road-style bodywork and long-travel suspension, and the very successful M900 Monster power cruiser, essentially a 900SS with an attitude, a tubular handlebar, and no fairing.

The Monster, originally built by Cagiva stylist Miguelangel Galluzzi as a styling exercise called Il Mostro, made it to production as much the result of

public acclaim as anything else. Basically a 900SS without fairing, British reporter Alan Cathcart rode the bike at the factory and fell in love with it. He wrote about it, and his enthusiastic reporting, which appeared in motorcycle magazines around the world, helped convince the factory that this two-wheeled hot rod had a future.

It certainly did. It became one of the company's most popular models, and it also became one of the machines most frequently modified, with many riders treating their machines to custom paint and to the wealth of bolt-on items an always-enthusiastic aftermarket offered them, and with some enthusiasts going as far as to install full-on Ducati Superbike engines in their Monsters. Monster, indeed.

Additionally, Ducati introduced in late 1994 the controversial eight-valve, fuel-injected 748 as a 600 Supersport-class bike. Almost completely identical to the 916 except in color and engine capacity, the 748 became part of the company's American sales plan for 1997, at a retail price about $3,000 less than that of the 916. This pricing is odd because, with the exception of just a few minor details, the 748 is identical to the 916, with exactly the same components and exactly the same build costs. The bike was developed to race in the very popular European 600 Supersport series, but was not accepted for racing in the United States in that class by the AMA.

Finally, at the 1996 Cologne IFMA Motorcycle Exposition, Ducati introduced a prototype ST2 sport-tourer, complete with integrated hard luggage, a tubular chassis much like that of the 916, and a 944-cc fuel-injected development of the 900SS engine.

All of this leaves Ducati, by 1997, right back at the same familiar straits. Its flagship bike, the 916, was three years old with no sign of a replacement. As this is written, a replacement engine design reportedly exists. But this design, if it does exist, was drawn without the budget to develop or build it. Ducati's other models also are in desperate need of upgrading in terms of styling and technical specification. Most are

powered by a derivative of the same air-cooled, four-valve, carbureted V-twin introduced at the 1990 IFMA show in the 900SS—which traces its roots back to the 1980 500 Pantah. Indeed, in 1997 Ducati finally showed an updated and restyled 900SS, but its arrival here in the United States remains unscheduled.

For all this model proliferation, and for all its racing successes—1996 marked Ducati's sixth manufacturer's championship in World Superbike—the company still teetered on the edge of cash-flow problems. Those problems appeared to be solved in late September 1996, when the Texas Pacific Group invested an

900SS REVISITED. Ducati, at the 1997 Milan show, finally introduced the third generation of a 900SS. Seen here on the factory's show stand, the bike bears little resemblance to its original progenitor but demonstrates the flare for style, shape, and proportion that marks Italian design.

undisclosed amount of money to buy a majority percentage of the company. As with everything at Ducati, this deal came along a curious and circuitous route.

In late 1995, rumors began circulating that Ducati was for sale. The Castiglionis had several good incentives for selling the company they had struggled so hard to make successful. The first was to get together a supply of ready cash. Ducati had become so strapped—observers claimed the brothers were using Ducati cash to pay off debts from their other companies—that it put suppliers on extended payment schedules. Suppliers responded by stopping the flow of critical components. Unable

to obtain things like wheels and bodywork, Ducati couldn't ship completed units. In fact, observers claim this was the reason it took Ducati all of 1994 to finally fill its delivery pipeline with 916s.

The second Castiglioni incentive involves the brothers' old dream of fielding a large-capacity motorcycle with the Cagiva name on it, making Cagiva, known for its small-capacity machines, a full-range manufacturer. After years of development and help from Ferrari, they were almost ready with a machine they called the Cagiva F4, a very Japanese-like machine powered by a cross-frame four-cylinder engine. Development money, however, was in short supply. One way to get it was to sell Ducati, which by then was enjoying reported worldwide sales of about $220 million annually.

The Castiglionis floated the possibility, and the first to rise to the bait was Chicago financier Sam Zell, a Ducati enthusiast who controls the Zell/Chilmark Fund. The deal fizzled for reasons not made public. Speculation, however, held that the deal crashed because the Castiglionis refused to sell a majority interest in the company, or because due-diligence studies revealed more Ducati debt than Zell was prepared to deal with, or because Zell's offer was too small, or all three.

The Castiglionis pitched Ducati again, and this time the Texas Pacific Group, which controls a reported $720 million in investment funds, stepped up to the plate. According to published reports, TPG paid $325 million for a 51 percent stake in Ducati, and agreed to a compromise that allows the Castiglionis to buy back 2 percent of the company. Some of these details are suspect, however. For instance, magazine reports had the deal closing on July 26, 1996, when in reality it wasn't complete until just before it was announced on September 30, 1996. Moreover, neither Texas Pacific nor Ducati ever released the specifics of the arrangement, and there was no sign that any reporter ever dug out detailed specifics of the deal.

Whatever the terms of the deal, Ducati's new investors made their presence felt. One of their first official acts was to terminate Vettore, sending him down the same road trod by Sandroni and the Carnellis. He remained unavailable for comment. Dan Van Epps, the company's marketing manager under Vettore, was elevated to the position of operations manager in what now is Ducati North America, with public relations manager Bruce Fairey elevated to the position of marketing manager.

Fairey says the mood at Ducati North America is positive and upbeat. And in the face of enthusiast concern that a group of investment bankers and their managers might not be able to master the intricacies of the motorcycle market—especially with a company like Ducati, with its exotic nature and its dependence on racing success—there also is faith that Ducati somehow will survive. Indeed, no less an observer than Phil Schilling said, "I think you've got to have some faith that come what may, there'll always be a Ducati."

Schilling is, of course, correct. All the signs point, finally, toward rational management of this most Italian of companies. Whether rational management can maintain the style, engineering excellence, and competition success Ducati needs in order to thrive remains to be seen. But even if the company fails to thrive, there will remain a hard core of enthusiasts in the United States and elsewhere who retain their passion and affection for the motorcycles of Ducati.

And on sunny, warm Sundays, garages from Miami to Seattle and from San Diego to Bangor will creak open. Bikes ranging from the early Singles to the latest 916s will be rolled out into the sunlight. They'll be started. And the profound beauty of their song, taught to them by Fabio Taglioni and arranged for modern ears by Massimo Bordi, will help ensure their continued existence. So will the purity of their line, from the oldest bikes to the newest. So will their crisp, taut feel once they start to roll.

And perhaps most important, so will their specific and individual character continue, the factor that so completely separates them from the homogeneous excellence, and the destructive sameness, of the committee-built world-bikes that swarm over the planet's best motorcycle roads. One way or another, Ducatis in America, in all their quirky Italian individuality, will remain a force to be reckoned with.

INDEX